CW00555860

VEGAN THAI
KITCHEN

VEGAN THAI KITCHEN

75 EASY AND DELICIOUS PLANT-BASED RECIPES WITH BOLD FLAVORS

SARAH JANSALA, CO-FOUNDER OF KATI PORTLAND

WITH RENOO JANSALA

PAGE STREET PUBLISHING CO.

First published in 2019 by

Page Street Publishing Co.

27 Congress Street, Suite 105

Salem, MA 01970

www.pagestreetpublishing.com

Distributed by Macmillan, sales in Canada by The Canadian Manda Group.

23 22 21 20 19 1 2 3 4 5

ISBN-13: 978-1-62414-900-9

ISBN-10: 1-62414-900-6

Library of Congress Control Number: 2019940336

Cover and book design by Laura Gallant for Page Street Publishing Co.

Photography by Toni Zernik

Printed and Bound in China

Page Street Publishing protects our planet by donating to nonprofits like The Trustees, which focuses on local land conservation.

TO MY PARENTS

Sukit and Renoo Jansala,
And sister, Suthaseenee Jansala,

Without whom none of my success would be possible.

CONTENTS

INTRODUCTION

Cooking has always been my passion. When I was young, I loved to watch my mom cook. I spent hours in the kitchen learning and helping her prepare food for the family. My mother is not only the first teacher in my life, but she is also the first person who introduced me to my love of cooking. Through cooking, my mother showed me how to value those moments when you patiently put things together dish by dish, and everybody says "WOW" at their first bite.

Later in adulthood, I found a deeper passion for cooking, and so in 2016 my business partner and I decided to open the first Thai vegetarian restaurant in Portland, Oregon, which we called Kati Portland. After two successful years, I took another step forward and started a Thai grab-and-go, plant-based juice bar and restaurant, called The Pear.

As a pharmacist and chef, I believe in the power of medicinal therapy as well as a healthy diet; both are necessary for the best results. We should always be aware of the quantity and quality of our food consumption every day. Everything we eat becomes a part of our body and therefore our health.

After years of collecting experiences and recipes, I'm now ready to share them with you. I believe everyone—from a beginner cook to an expert chef—should be able to make and share my love of Thai food with their family and also start living a healthier life.

Co-founder of Kati Portland

Founder of The Pear and Thai Home Curry Paste

SIMPLE AND CLASSIC THAI STIR-FRY, SOFT TOFU **AND MORE**

There are many types of Thai main dishes, including stir-fries, fried rice, salads and curries, but stir-fries are the most popular because they are easy, delicious and fast during a busy workweek. They are also a popular street food in Thailand.

Most Thai food features vegetables as the main ingredients, so it's a cuisine that is simple to make vegan. I love using tofu, tempeh, soy curls and veggie meat as proteins. Thai-style main dishes are commonly served with steamed jasmine rice and side dishes as part of a family meal.

In this chapter, I try to make it simple, fast and delicious. Most recipes should take less than 15 to 20 minutes to make. Enjoy!

SWEET AND SOUR TEMPEH

(PAD PREAW WAHN)

When it comes to simple Thai recipes, Sweet and Sour Tempeh is a winner. This dish is full of vegetables and tempeh, meaning it contains protein, vitamins, fiber and minerals! Sweet and sour tempeh is basically pan-fried tempeh and mixed vegetables stir-fried with a mouthwatering sweet and sour sauce.

SERVES 4

PREAW WAHN SAUCE

4 tbsp (60 ml) tamari

3 tbsp (45 ml) apple cider vinegar

¾ cup (180 g) ketchup

¼ cup (55 g) brown sugar

8 tbsp (120 ml) vegetable oil, divided

9 oz (255 g) tempeh, cut into sticks ½" x 2" (1.3 x 5 cm)

1 tsp minced garlic

¼ cup (60 ml) vegetable broth

½ red bell pepper, cut into 1" (2.5-cm) squares

½ green bell pepper, cut into 1" (2.5-cm) squares

½ yellow onion, cut into 1" (2.5-cm) squares

1 cup (130 g) 1" (2.5-cm) cubed English cucumber (seedless)

2 cups (362 g) chopped pineapple

3 green onions, cut into 2" (5-cm) lengths

Steamed jasmine rice, for serving

To make the sauce, combine the tamari, vinegar, ketchup and brown sugar in a small bowl and stir well until the sugar is dissolved.

Heat 6 tablespoons (90 ml) of the oil in a pan over medium heat, add the tempeh and fry on each side for about 3 minutes or until all the sides are golden brown. Remove from the pan and drain well.

Add the remaining 2 tablespoons (30 ml) of vegetable oil to the pan and heat over medium heat. Add the garlic and fry until golden brown, about 1 minute. Add the sauce and vegetable broth to the pan and increase the heat to high. Add the red and green bell peppers, onion, cucumber, pineapple, green onions and tempeh, and stir until well combined and the vegetables have softened, about 1 minute.

Serve with steamed jasmine rice.

STIR-FRIED TARO AND POTATO WITH DRIED CHILES

(PAD MED MA MUANG HIMMAPARN)

This popular dish is considered an expensive one at most restaurants due to having cashew nuts as an ingredient. In this easy and beautiful recipe, fried tofu and colorful vegetables are tossed in a flavorful, sweet and salty sauce and topped with freshly roasted cashews.

SERVES 4

SAUCE

2 tbsp (30 ml) tamari

2 tbsp (30 ml) mushroom stir-fry sauce

2 tbsp (28 g) brown sugar

1 cup (150 g) 1" (2.5-cm) cubed taro

1 cup (150 g) 1" (2.5-cm) cubed potato

8 tbsp (120 ml) vegetable oil, divided

8 oz (228 g) firm tofu, cut into 1" (2.5-cm) squares

8 dried chiles

1 tsp minced garlic

½ yellow onion, cut into 1" (2.5-cm) squares

½ red bell pepper, cut into 1" (2.5-cm) squares

½ green bell pepper, cut into 1" (2.5-cm) squares

1 cup (128 g) sliced carrot

4 dried shiitake mushrooms, soaked in warm water, drained and quartered

2 tbsp (30 ml) vegetable broth

3 tbsp (27 g) whole cashews or peanuts

Steamed jasmine rice, for serving

To make the sauce, combine the tamari, mushroom stir-fry sauce and brown sugar in a small bowl and mix until well combined and the sugar has dissolved.

Bring a small pot of water to a boil over medium-high heat, add the taro and potato and cook for 8 minutes. Drain and let cool.

Heat 6 tablespoons (90 ml) of the oil in a pan over medium heat, add the tofu and fry for 3 minutes on each side, until all the sides are lightly browned. Remove from the pan and drain well.

Heat the remaining 2 tablespoons (30 ml) of oil in a pan over medium heat, add the chiles and fry until crispy, 20 to 30 seconds. Remove from the pan and let cool. Add the garlic to the pan and fry for 10 seconds. Add the onion, red and green bell peppers, carrot, shiitake mushrooms and broth to the pan and cook, stirring, until well combined and the vegetables have softened, about 1 minute. Add the fried tofu, season with the sauce mixture and heat through. Top with the crispy chiles and whole cashews.

Serve with steamed jasmine rice.

SPICY BASIL TEMPEH

(PAD KRAPRAO)

If you cannot make up your mind about what to eat for lunch, Pad Kraprao is your simply delicious solution. It is one of the most popular Thai street foods for office workers. The key ingredients are Thai basil, garlic, chile and your choice of protein. There are two different types of Thai basil that can be used: regular Thai basil and holy Thai basil. I find that holy Thai basil has a wonderful fragrance and delicious peppery taste, but it is not easy to find. Regular Thai basil is delicious as well.

SERVES 4

SAUCE

2 tbsp (30 ml) tamari

2 tbsp (30 ml) mushroom stir-fry sauce

2 tbsp (28 g) brown sugar

8 tbsp (120 ml) vegetable oil, divided

9 oz (255 g) tempeh, cut into ½" x 2" (1.3 x 5–cm) sticks

4 Thai chiles, finely chopped

2 tsp (6 g) minced garlic

6 button mushrooms, halved

½ red bell pepper, cut into 1" (2.5-cm) squares

½ green bell pepper, cut into 1" (2.5-cm) squares

½ yellow onion, cut into 1" (2.5-cm) squares

1 cup (128 g) sliced carrot

7 green beans, cut into 2" (5-cm) lengths

2 tbsp (30 ml) vegetable broth

2 green onions, cut into 2" (5-cm) lengths

2 handfuls of Thai sweet basil

To make the sauce, combine the tamari, mushroom stir-fry sauce and brown sugar in a small bowl and mix until well combined and the sugar has dissolved.

Heat 6 tablespoons (90 ml) of the oil in a pan over medium heat, add the tempeh and fry on each side for about 3 minutes or until all the sides are golden brown. Remove from the pan and drain well.

Add the remaining 2 tablespoons (30 ml) of vegetable oil to the pan and heat over medium heat. Add the chiles and garlic and fry until golden brown, about 10 seconds. Add the mushrooms, red and green bell peppers, yellow onion, carrot, green beans and vegetable broth and stir. Cook until well combined and the vegetables have softened, about 1 minute. Add the tempeh, green onions and basil, season with the sauce mixture and stir for 30 seconds to heat through.

SPICY EGGPLANT

(PAD MAKHUEA)

Eggplant is used in a variety of Thai dishes, especially red curries, and its meaty texture is perfect for vegan recipes. It is most often grilled, stir-fried or deep-fried. In this recipe, we cut the eggplant into rounds and then fry them until they're half cooked before tossing them into the stir-fry mixture. The three key ingredients for this dish are eggplant, basil and soybean paste; tofu adds the protein.

SERVES 4

SAUCE

2 tbsp (30 ml) tamari

2 tbsp (30 ml) mushroom stir-fry sauce

2 tbsp (28 g) brown sugar

1 tsp soybean paste (taojeaw)

8 tbsp (120 ml) vegetable oil, divided, plus more as needed

8 oz (228 g) firm tofu, cut into 1" (2.5-cm) squares

2 long Chinese eggplant, cut into 1" (2.5-cm)-thick rounds

4 Thai chiles, finely chopped

1 tsp minced garlic

½ yellow onion, cut into 1" (2.5-cm) squares

½ red bell pepper, cut into 1" (2.5-cm) squares

½ green bell pepper, cut into 1" (2.5-cm) squares

1 cup (128 g) sliced carrot

2 tbsp (30 ml) vegetable broth

2 green onions, cut into 2" (5-cm) lengths

2 handfuls of Thai sweet basil

To make the sauce, combine the tamari, mushroom stir-fry sauce, brown sugar and soybean paste in a small bowl and mix until well combined and the sugar has dissolved.

Heat 6 tablespoons (90 ml) of the oil in a pan over medium heat and fry the tofu for 3 minutes on each side until all the sides are golden brown. Remove from the pan and drain. If needed, add more oil to the pan and fry the eggplant on each side for about 3 minutes or until both sides are golden brown. Remove from the pan and drain well.

Add the remaining 2 tablespoons (30 ml) of oil to a clean pan over medium heat, add the chiles and garlic and fry until golden brown, about 10 seconds. Add the onion, red and green bell peppers, carrot and vegetable broth and cook, stirring, until well combined and the vegetables have softened, about 1 minute. Add the fried tofu, fried eggplant, green onions and basil, season with the sauce mixture and stir for 30 seconds to heat through.

VEGETABLE MEDLEY

(PAD PAK)

This is a very easy recipe and a delicious dish to prepare. If you don't have time to shop around for the vegetables called for, simply use what you have on hand. You may discover a new favorite healthy dinner for the family. Serve with steamed jasmine rice.

SERVES 4

SAUCE

2 tbsp (30 ml) tamari

2 tbsp (30 ml) mushroom stir-fry sauce

2 tbsp (28 g) brown sugar

8 tbsp (120 ml) vegetable oil, divided

2 oz (57 g) firm tofu, cut into 1" (2.5-cm) squares

1 tsp minced garlic

½ yellow onion, cut into 1" (2.5-cm) squares

1 cup (128 g) sliced carrot

8 button mushrooms, halved

3 cups (210 g) shredded cabbage

10 grape tomatoes

1 cup (63 g) snow peas

½ red bell pepper, cut into 1" (2.5-cm) squares

½ green bell pepper, cut into 1" (2.5-cm) squares

2 tbsp (30 ml) vegetable broth

2 green onions, cut into 2" (5-cm) lengths

Steamed jasmine rice, for serving

To make the sauce, combine the tamari, mushroom stir-fry sauce and brown sugar in a small bowl and mix until well combined and the sugar has dissolved.

Heat 6 tablespoons (90 ml) of the oil in a pan over medium heat and fry the tofu on each side for about 3 minutes or until all the sides are golden brown. Remove from the pan and drain well.

Add the remaining 2 tablespoons (30 ml) of oil to the pan and heat over medium heat. Add the garlic and fry until golden brown, about 10 seconds. Add the yellow onion, carrot, mushrooms, cabbage, tomatoes, snow peas, red and green bell peppers and vegetable broth and cook, stirring, until well combined and the vegetables have softened, about 1 minute. Add the fried tofu and green onions, season with the sauce mixture and stir for 30 seconds to heat through.

Serve with steamed jasmine rice.

GARLIC AND PEPPER TOFU

This quick tofu stir-fry is another popular street food that is perfect for a quick lunch. You can make this dish with your choice of protein, such as tempeh, soy curls or veggie meat, instead of the tofu, but you must make sure the protein is nice and crispy before tossing it in the garlic and pepper sauce.

SERVES 4

SAUCE

1½ tbsp (23 ml) tamari

1½ tbsp (23 ml) mushroom stir-fry sauce

1½ tbsp (21 g) brown sugar

½ tsp ground black pepper

½ cup plus 2 tbsp (150 ml) vegetable oil, divided

16 oz (456 g) firm tofu, cut into 1" (2.5-cm) squares

8 tbsp (64 g) minced garlic

Steamed jasmine rice, for serving

To make the sauce, combine the tamari, mushroom stir-fry sauce, brown sugar and pepper in a small bowl and mix until well combined and the sugar has dissolved.

Heat ½ cup (120 ml) of the oil in a deep pan over medium heat, add the tofu and fry for 3 minutes on each side until all the sides are lightly browned. Remove from the pan and drain well. Use the same oil to fry the minced garlic until crispy and golden brown, about 1 to 2 minutes, then remove from the pan and drain well.

Heat the remaining 2 tablespoons (30 ml) of oil in the pan over low heat, add the sauce mixture and stir well. Toss in the fried tofu and cook until all the sides are covered by the sauce, 1 to 2 minutes. Top with the crispy fried garlic to serve.

Serve with steamed jasmine rice.

TIP: After completely draining out the oil, spread the fried garlic on a paper towel to dry and cool the garlic. This process will make the garlic nice and crunchy.

GINGER TOFU

(PAD KHING)

This recipe is perfect for those who love the flavor and heat of ginger, or khing *in Thai. This classic quick and simple recipe is influenced by Chinese food. This dish is also one of my childhood favorites. A comforting, fragrant dish that is healthy and easy to make, it features a unique garlic-mushroom sauce.*

SERVES 4

SAUCE

2 tbsp (30 ml) tamari

2 tbsp (30 ml) mushroom stir-fry sauce

2 tbsp (28 g) brown sugar

1 tsp soybean paste (taojeaw)

8 tbsp (120 ml) vegetable oil, divided

8 oz (228 g) firm tofu, cut into 1" (2.5-cm) squares

1 tbsp (8 g) minced garlic

½ yellow onion, cut into 1" (2.5-cm) squares

½ red bell pepper, cut into 1" (2.5-cm) squares

½ green bell pepper, cut into 1" (2.5-cm) squares

1 cup (128 g) sliced carrot

8 button mushrooms, halved

2 tbsp (30 ml) vegetable broth

2 green onions, cut into 2" (5-cm) lengths

1 cup (101 g) sliced celery

¼ cup (24 g) finely sliced ginger

Steamed jasmine rice, for serving

To make the sauce, combine the tamari, mushroom stir-fry sauce, brown sugar and soybean paste in a small bowl and mix until well combined and the sugar has dissolved.

Heat 6 tablespoons (90 ml) of the oil in a pan over medium heat, add the tofu and fry for 3 minutes on each side until all the sides are lightly browned. Remove from the pan and drain well.

Heat the remaining 2 tablespoons (30 ml) of oil in the pan over medium heat, add the garlic and fry until golden brown, about 10 seconds, then add the yellow onion, red and green bell peppers, carrot, mushrooms and vegetable broth and cook, stirring, until well combined and the vegetables have softened, about 1 minute. Add the fried tofu, green onions, celery and ginger, season with the sauce mixture and stir for 30 seconds to heat through.

Serve with steamed jasmine rice.

JUNGLE CURRY STIR-FRY

(PAD CHA)

Pad cha means *"sizzling stir-fry," and it is the sound when the ingredients hit the hot pan or wok. This recipe is a perfect blend of Thai herbs and spices, and it will make your kitchen smell wonderful. The key ingredient, red curry paste, can be found at most supermarkets and online stores, but make sure you get one that has no shrimp paste, as many of them contain shellfish products. If you like a hot and spicy stir-fry, do not miss putting this on the menu!*

SERVES 4

SAUCE

2 tbsp (30 ml) tamari

2 tbsp (30 ml) mushroom stir-fry sauce

2 tbsp (28 g) brown sugar

3 tbsp (45 ml) vegetable oil

6 oz (171 g) firm tofu, cut into 1" (2.5-cm) squares

6 oz (171 g) kabocha squash, peeled and cut into ½" (1.3-cm) squares

5 Thai eggplants, halved

1 tbsp (15 ml) coconut oil

1½ tbsp (23 g) vegan Thai red curry paste

2 tbsp (30 ml) vegetable broth

6 kaffir lime leaves

½ red bell pepper, cut into 1" (2.5-cm) squares

½ green bell pepper, cut into 1" (2.5-cm) squares

½ cup (76 g) sliced bamboo shoot

4 peppercorn stalks

7 whole baby corn

3 button mushrooms, halved

½ cup (32 g) snow peas, halved

1 handful of Thai basil

To make the sauce, combine the tamari, mushroom stir-fry sauce and brown sugar in a small bowl and mix until well combined and the sugar has dissolved.

Heat the vegetable oil in a pan over medium heat, add the tofu and fry on each side for about 3 minutes or until all the sides are golden brown. Remove from the pan and drain well.

Bring a small pot of water to a boil over medium-high heat, add the kabocha squash and Thai eggplants and cook for 8 minutes. Drain and let cool.

Heat the coconut oil in a large saucepan over medium heat, add the red curry paste and cook, stirring, for about 1 minute, then add the vegetable broth and stir until well combined. Add the kabocha squash, lime leaves, red and green bell peppers, bamboo shoot, eggplants, peppercorn stalks, baby corn and mushrooms and increase the heat to high. Cook, stirring, until well combined and the vegetables have softened, about 1 minute. Add the fried tofu, snow peas and basil, season with the sauce mixture and stir for 30 seconds to heat through.

GLASS NOODLES WITH MIXED VEGETABLES

(PAD WOON SEN)

Woon sen, or glass noodles, are made from mung bean flour. This type of noodle is very low in calories, which makes this dish a healthy noodle recipe. Because it has a simple flavor and is light on spice, it's popular with children. For adults, if you like things spicy, you can always add chile pepper or a few drops of chile oil.

SERVES 4

SAUCE

2 tbsp (30 ml) tamari

2 tbsp (30 ml) mushroom stir-fry sauce

2 tbsp (28 g) brown sugar

½ tsp black pepper

7 oz (200 g) Thai mung bean noodles

5 tbsp (75 ml) vegetable oil, divided

4 oz (114 g) firm tofu, cut into 1" (2.5-cm) squares

1 tsp minced garlic

¼ yellow onion, cut into 1" (2.5-cm) squares

1 cup (128 g) sliced carrot

8 button mushrooms, halved

2 cups (140 g) shredded cabbage

6 grape tomatoes

1 cup (63 g) snow peas

½ red bell pepper, cut into 1" (2.5-cm) squares

½ green bell pepper, cut into 1" (2.5-cm) squares

¼ cup (60 ml) vegetable broth

2 green onions, cut into 2" (5-cm) lengths

To make the sauce, combine the tamari, mushroom stir-fry sauce, brown sugar and black pepper in a small bowl and mix until well combined and the sugar has dissolved.

Soak the noodles in cold water for about 10 minutes, drain and cut into 6-inch (15-cm) lengths.

Heat 3 tablespoons (45 ml) of the oil in a pan over medium heat, add the tofu and fry on each side for about 3 minutes, or until all the sides are golden brown. Remove from the pan and drain well.

Add the remaining 2 tablespoons (30 ml) of oil to the pan and heat over medium heat, then add the garlic and fry until golden brown, about 10 seconds. Add the yellow onion, carrot, mushrooms, cabbage, tomatoes, snow peas, red and green bell peppers, glass noodles and vegetable broth and cook, stirring, until well combined and the vegetables have softened, about 1 minute. Add the fried tofu and green onions, season with the sauce mixture and stir for 30 seconds to heat through.

SOFT TOFU YELLOW CURRY STIR-FRY

(TAO HOO PAD PONG KAREE)

This dish features tofu that is cooked together with a curry sauce made of yellow curry powder, coconut cream and tamari. Green and yellow onions and red and green bell peppers add color, freshness and texture to the dish. It tastes amazing and looks great on top of steamed jasmine rice. This is an ideal dish if you would like to make a quick and easy stir-fry curry meal!

SERVES 4

SAUCE

2 tbsp (30 ml) tamari

2 tbsp (30 ml) mushroom stir-fry sauce

2 tbsp (28 g) brown sugar

2 tsp (4 g) yellow curry powder

1 tbsp (16 g) vegan Thai sweet chili paste (nam prik pao)

12 oz (342 g) soft tofu

2 tbsp (30 ml) vegetable oil

2 tsp (6 g) minced garlic

½ yellow onion, cut into 1" (2.5-cm) squares

½ red bell pepper, cut into 1" (2.5-cm) squares

½ green bell pepper, cut into 1" (2.5-cm) squares

¼ cup (60 ml) vegetable broth

¼ cup (60 ml) coconut cream

½ cup (50 g) chopped green onion

Steamed jasmine rice, for serving

To make the sauce, combine the tamari, mushroom stir-fry sauce, brown sugar, yellow curry powder and chile paste in a small bowl and mix until well combined and the sugar has dissolved.

Bring a small pot of water to a boil over medium-high heat, add the soft tofu and cook for 1 minute, then drain and let cool. Place the soft tofu on a serving plate.

Heat the vegetable oil in a pan over medium heat, add the garlic and fry until golden brown, about 10 seconds. Add the yellow onion, red and green bell peppers and vegetable broth and cook, stirring, until well combined and the vegetables have softened, about 1 minute. Add the coconut cream and green onion and season with the sauce mixture, then cook for another minute. Place the vegetables on top of the steamed soft tofu and serve with jasmine rice.

PORTOBELLO MUSHROOMS WITH SOFT TOFU

Portobello mushrooms are a good source of protein. With their unique texture and flavor, portobellos can be cooked in a variety of ways, including in a curry, stir-fried, grilled or deep-fried. I find that simply stir-frying portobellos with tofu and a garlic-tamari sauce brings out their meaty flavor perfectly.

SERVES 4

SAUCE

1½ tbsp (23 ml) tamari

1½ tbsp (23 ml) mushroom sir-fry sauce

1½ tbsp (21 g) brown sugar

2 tbsp (30 ml) vegetable oil

2 tsp (6 g) minced garlic

2 portobello mushrooms, cut into bite-size pieces

1 cup (128 g) diced carrot

1 tbsp (15 ml) vegetable broth

8 oz (228 g) soft tofu, cut into 1" (2.5-cm) squares

¾ cup (75 g) 1" (2.5-cm)-long sliced green onion

Steamed jasmine rice, for serving

To make the sauce, combine the tamari, mushroom stir-fry sauce and brown sugar in a small bowl and mix until well combined and the sugar has dissolved.

Heat the oil in a pan over medium heat, add the garlic and fry until golden brown, about 10 seconds. Add the mushrooms, carrot and broth and cook, stirring, until combined and the vegetables have softened, about 2 minutes. Add the soft tofu and green onion, season with the sauce mixture and cook for 1½ minutes.

Serve with steamed jasmine rice.

TIP: Add about ¼ teaspoon of ground chile powder for some heat.

TOFU WITH CELERY IN GINGER SAUCE

I transformed this recipe from a dish called Pad Pla Keun Chai, a stir-fried fish fillet with ginger and Chinese celery. You will be amazed by the flavor when we use tofu or tempeh in this dish instead of fish. My favorite way of eating this dish is with a bowl of hot rice soup, which is really satisfying on a cold winter day.

SERVES 4

SAUCE

1½ tbsp (23 ml) tamari

1½ tbsp (23 ml) mushroom stir-fry sauce

1 tsp soybean paste (taojeaw)

1½ tbsp (21 g) brown sugar

2 tbsp (30 ml) vegetable oil

2 tsp (6 g) minced garlic

2 cups (202 g) 1½" (3.8-cm)-long chopped Chinese celery

½ cup (32 g) julienned carrot

¼ red bell pepper, julienned

¼ green bell pepper, julienned

2 tbsp (16 g) finely julienned ginger

1 tbsp (15 ml) vegetable broth

8 oz (228 g) soft tofu, cut into 1" (2.5-cm) squares

To make the sauce, combine the tamari, mushroom stir-fry sauce, soybean paste and brown sugar in a small bowl and mix until well combined and the sugar has dissolved.

Heat the oil in a pan over medium heat, add the garlic and fry until golden brown, about 10 seconds. Add the celery, carrot, red and green bell peppers, ginger and broth and cook, stirring, until well combined and the vegetables have softened, about 30 seconds. Add the soft tofu, season with the sauce and cook for 1½ minutes.

SWEET AND SOUR CRISPY SEAWEED TOFU

(PAD PREAW WAHN)

The crispy seaweed tofu is supposed to imitate the crispy fried fish in many Thai recipes. Let's call it "vegan fish." Stir-fried pineapple, cucumber, bell peppers and onions in a sweet and sour, savory tomato sauce are placed on top of the crispy seaweed-wrapped tofu. This dish is full of flavors and tons of veggies that you must try!

SERVES 4

PREAW WAHN SAUCE

4 tbsp (60 ml) tamari

3 tbsp (45 ml) apple cider vinegar

¾ cup (180 g) ketchup

¼ cup (55 g) brown sugar

¼ cup (60 ml) water

4 tbsp (32 g) cornstarch

4 sheets nori seaweed

4 oz (114 g) firm tofu, cut into 4" x 1½" (10 x 3.8-cm) sticks

5 tbsp (75 ml) vegetable oil, divided

4 tbsp (32 g) rice flour

1 tsp minced garlic

¼ cup (60 ml) vegetable broth

½ red bell pepper, cut into 1" (2.5-cm) squares

½ green bell pepper, cut into 1" (2.5-cm) squares

½ yellow onion, cut into 1" (2.5-cm) squares

2 cups (362 g) chopped pineapple

1 cup (130 g) chopped English cucumber

3 green onions, cut into 2" (5-cm) lengths

Steamed jasmine rice, for serving

To make the sauce, combine the tamari, apple cider vinegar, ketchup and brown sugar in a small bowl and stir until well combined and the sugar has dissolved.

Mix the water and cornstarch in a small bowl to use as an adhesive agent.

Lay a seaweed wrapper flat on your work surface and place one piece of tofu on one end. Roll up the seaweed wrapper, enclosing the tofu, and seal the edge by dipping your finger in the cornstarch mixture and then running it along the edge of the seaweed. Repeat with the remaining seaweed and tofu.

Heat 3 tablespoons (45 ml) of the oil in a pan over medium heat, coat the tofu packets with rice flour and fry gently on all sides until they turn crispy and golden brown but are still soft on the inside, about 8 minutes on each side. Drain well and let cool. Place on a serving plate.

Add the remaining 2 tablespoons (30 ml) of oil to the pan and heat over medium heat, then add the garlic and fry until golden brown, 10 seconds. Add the sauce and vegetable broth to the pan and increase the heat to high. Add the red and green bell peppers, yellow onion, pineapple, cucumber and green onions and cook, stirring, until well combined and the vegetables have softened, about 1 minute. Serve the vegetables over the crispy seaweed tofu.

Serve immediately with steamed jasmine rice.

PANANG CRISPY SEAWEED TOFU

(CHUHEE)

Panang curry sauce is always a good choice for crispy seaweed tofu. It is pretty similar to red curry, but Panang curry is thick, creamy and usually less spicy than traditional red curry. It also has a unique flavor and fragrance from the addition of kaffir lime leaves and other herbs. The combination of the crispy seaweed tofu and the Panang curry sauce will make you ask for an extra bowl of rice!

SERVES 4

- **4 tbsp (60 ml) water**
- **4 tbsp (32 g) cornstarch**
- **4 sheets nori seaweed**
- **4 oz (114 g) firm tofu, cut into 4" x 1½" (10 x 3.8-cm) sticks**
- **6 tbsp (90 ml) vegetable oil**
- **4 tbsp (32 g) rice flour**
- **1 tbsp (15 ml) coconut oil**
- **1½ tbsp (23 g) vegan Thai Panang curry paste**
- **2 cups (480 ml) coconut milk**
- **½ red bell pepper, cut into 1" (2.5-cm) squares**
- **½ green bell pepper, cut into 1" (2.5-cm) squares**
- **2 tbsp (17 g) peppercorns (optional)**
- **¼ cup (55 g) brown sugar**
- **¼ cup (60 ml) tamari**
- **2 handfuls of Thai basil**
- **Steamed jasmine rice, for serving**
- **2 tbsp (16 g) shredded kaffir lime leaves**

Mix the water and cornstarch in a small bowl to use as an adhesive agent.

Lay a seaweed wrapper flat on your work surface and place one piece of the tofu on one end. Roll up the seaweed wrapper, enclosing the tofu, and seal the edge by dipping your finger in the cornstarch mixture and then running it along the edge of the seaweed. Repeat with the remaining seaweed and tofu.

Heat the vegetable oil in a pan over medium heat, coat the tofu packets with rice flour and fry gently on all sides until they turn crispy and golden brown but are still soft on the inside, about 8 minutes on each side. Drain well and let cool. Place on a serving plate.

Heat the coconut oil in a large saucepan over medium heat, add the Panang curry paste and stir for about 1 minute, then add the coconut milk and stir until well combined. Heat the mixture for a few more minutes or until the oil begins to separate. Add the red and green bell peppers and peppercorns, if using, increase the heat to high and bring the mixture to a boil. Once it's boiling, add the sugar, tamari and Thai basil and simmer for 1 minute. Serve the vegetables over the crispy seaweed tofu with a side of rice and sprinkle with the lime leaves.

TIP: This dish is best eaten immediately to maintain the crispy texture of the seaweed.

THREE-FLAVORED CRISPY SEAWEED TOFU

This recipe is a rendition of Three-Flavored Fish (Pla Sam Rod), a specialty fish dish in Thailand, so named because the sauce has three distinct flavors: sweet, sour and spicy. If you know how to make the Three-Flavored Sauce, you will also know how to create many more dishes. I like to use it for tossing vegetable tempura right out of the fryer. Serve with steamed rice or steamed rice noodles.

SERVES 4

¼ cup (60 ml) water

4 tbsp (32 g) cornstarch

4 sheets nori seaweed

4 oz (114 g) firm tofu, cut into 4" x 1½" (10 x 3.8-cm) sticks

5 tbsp (75 ml) vegetable oil, divided

4 tbsp (32 g) rice flour

½ red bell pepper, cut into 1" (2.5-cm) squares

½ green bell pepper, cut into 1" (2.5-cm) squares

½ yellow onion, cut into 1" (2.5-cm) squares

THREE-FLAVORED SAUCE

2 tbsp (30 ml) vegetable oil

2 tbsp (16 g) minced garlic

6 Thai chiles, finely chopped

½ cup (110 g) brown sugar

¼ cup (60 ml) water

¼ cup (60 ml) apple cider vinegar

2 tbsp (30 ml) tamarind juice

2 tbsp (30 ml) tamari

1 tsp salt

Mix the water and cornstarch in a small bowl to use as an adhesive agent.

Lay a seaweed wrapper flat on your work surface and place one piece of the tofu on one end. Roll up the seaweed wrapper, enclosing the tofu, and seal the edge by dipping your finger in the cornstarch mixture and then running it along the edge of the seaweed. Repeat with the remaining seaweed and tofu.

Heat 3 tablespoons (45 ml) of the vegetable oil in a pan over medium heat, coat the tofu packets with rice flour and fry gently on all sides until they turn crispy and golden brown but are still soft on the inside, about 8 minutes on each side. Drain well and let cool. Place on a serving plate.

Add the remaining 2 tablespoons (30 ml) of oil to the pan and place over medium heat. Add the red and green bell peppers and yellow onion and cook, stirring, for 1 minute, then place the vegetables on the crispy seaweed tofu.

To make the sauce, heat the oil in a pan over medium heat, add the garlic and chiles and fry until golden brown, about 10 seconds. Add the brown sugar, water, apple cider vinegar, tamarind juice, tamari and salt and stir until the sugar has dissolved and the sauce has thickened, 1 minute. Drizzle the sauce on top of the vegetables and crispy tofu.

TIP: This dish is best eaten immediately to maintain the crispy texture of the seaweed.

CRISPY SEAWEED TOFU

(PRIK KHING)

If you haven't tasted Prik Khing, a drier type of Thai curry that is stir-fried and does not contain coconut milk, you should try this recipe. The two keys ingredients are vegan Thai red curry paste and tamari, making this dish spicy, sweet and savory all at once.

SERVES 4

PRIK KHING SAUCE

2 tbsp (30 ml) tamari

2 tbsp (30 ml) mushroom stir-fry sauce

2 tbsp (28 g) brown sugar

1½ tbsp (23 g) vegan Thai red curry paste

¼ cup (60 ml) water

4 tbsp (32 g) cornstarch

4 sheets nori seaweed

4 oz (114 g) firm tofu, cut into 4" x 1½" (10 x 3.8–cm) sticks

5 tbsp (75 ml) vegetable oil, divided

4 tbsp (32 g) rice flour

1 cup (63 g) sugar snap peas

½ red bell pepper, cut into 1" (2.5-cm) squares

½ green bell pepper, cut into 1" (2.5-cm) squares

1 tbsp (3 g) shredded kaffir lime leaves

1 tbsp (14 g) shredded ginger

2 handfuls of Thai basil

To make the sauce, combine the tamari, mushroom stir-fry sauce, brown sugar and red curry paste in a small bowl and mix until well combined and the sugar has dissolved.

Mix the water and cornstarch in a small bowl to use as an adhesive agent.

Lay a seaweed wrapper flat on your work surface and place half the tofu on one end. Roll up the seaweed wrapper, enclosing the tofu, and seal the edge by dipping your finger in the cornstarch mixture and then running it along the edge of the seaweed. Repeat with the remaining seaweed and tofu.

Heat 3 tablespoons (45 ml) of the oil in a pan over medium heat, coat the tofu packets with rice flour and fry gently on all sides until they turn crispy golden brown but are still soft on the inside, about 8 minutes on each side. Drain well and let cool. Place on a serving plate.

Add the remaining 2 tablespoons (30 ml) of oil to the pan over medium heat, add the sauce mixture, sugar snap peas, red and green bell peppers, lime leaves, ginger and basil and sauté for 30 seconds, then pour on top of the crispy tofu.

TIP: This dish is best eaten immediately to maintain the crispy texture of the seaweed.

FAST AND EASY GLUTEN-FREE NOODLES AND FRIED RICE

Rice is the main source of carbohydrates in many countries, including Thailand. It is well known that Thai white rice and Thai glutinous rice can be processed into rice flour, and rice flour is used to create various dishes as well as rice noodles. Not only are these noodles delicious, they're also gluten-free.

There are many Thai street food dishes made from rice and noodles that you can easily find at any street corner in Thailand. One of the most popular Thai noodle dishes is pad Thai, not only because it is easy to make but because it is delicious as well.

In this chapter, we are going to use a lot of tamari. The reason why is because it lends a savory flavor with less salt, and it also has gluten-free (wheat-free) options available. If you don't mind having dishes containing gluten, then regular soy sauce can be substituted.

GLUTEN-FREE THREE MUSHROOM NOODLES

(PAD MEEH KHANA)

This thin rice noodle dish with Chinese broccoli is one of the popular vegan dishes found during the vegan festival in Thailand. Chinese broccoli can be found at most Asian supermarkets, but if you can't find it, regular broccoli or kale can be used instead. Because it has a light flavor and is less spicy, this dish has been a popular menu item for most children who visit us at Kati Portland restaurant.

SERVES 4

SAUCE

2 tbsp (30 ml) gluten-free tamari

2 tbsp (30 ml) mushroom stir-fry sauce

2 tbsp (28 g) brown sugar

½ tsp black pepper

2 tbsp (30 ml) vegetable oil

1 tsp minced garlic

½ yellow onion, cut into 1" (2.5-cm) squares

½ cup (64 g) sliced carrot

10 white mushrooms, halved

10 cremini mushrooms, halved

10 shiitake mushrooms, halved

25 oz (709 g) angel hair rice noodles, cooked per package directions

10 grape tomatoes

2 tbsp (30 ml) vegetable broth

8 stalks of Chinese broccoli (or regular broccoli), cut into 2" (5-cm) lengths

To make the sauce, combine the tamari, mushroom stir-fry sauce, brown sugar and black pepper in a small bowl and mix until well combined and the sugar has dissolved.

Add the vegetable oil to a pan and heat over medium heat, then add the garlic and fry until golden brown, 10 seconds. Add the yellow onion, carrot and mushrooms and cook, stirring, until the vegetables have softened, 1 minute. Add the noodles, tomatoes, vegetable broth and sauce mixture, and stir to make sure the noodles are coated. Stir for a few minutes, until the sauce soaks into the noodles, then add the Chinese broccoli and cook for 30 seconds more (if using regular broccoli, cook for 1 minute).

12

GLUTEN-FREE PAD THAI

The world-famous noodle dish pad Thai can now be served gluten-free. Pad in Thai means "stir-fry." Different regions of Thailand have their own style of pad Thai. In this recipe, we will make pad Thai that is seasoned with gluten-free tamari, lime juice, brown sugar, paprika and apple cider vinegar. Pad Thai is traditionally served with lime wedges, chopped roasted peanuts and fresh garlic chives.

SERVES 4

SAUCE

½ cup (120 ml) gluten-free tamari

1 tbsp (15 ml) lime juice

½ cup plus 2 tbsp (138 g) brown sugar

2 tsp (4 g) paprika

2 tbsp (30 ml) apple cider vinegar

¾ cup (180 ml) water

5 tbsp (75 ml) vegetable oil, divided

6 oz (171 g) firm tofu, cut into ½" (1.3-cm) squares

8 tbsp (80 g) sliced shallot

18 oz (510 g) pad Thai noodles, soaked in cold water for 1 hour and drained

3 cup (300 g) bean sprouts

¾ cup (36 g) sliced garlic chives (or green onion)

6 tbsp (60 g) crushed peanuts, for garnish

Lime wedges, for serving

Chile powder, for serving

To make the sauce, combine the tamari, lime juice, brown sugar, paprika, apple cider vinegar and water in a small bowl and stir until well combined and the sugar has dissolved.

Heat 3 tablespoons (45 ml) of the oil in a pan over medium heat, add the tofu and fry for about 3 minutes on each side until all the sides are lightly browned. Remove from the pan and drain well. Use the same oil to fry the shallot until golden brown, about 8 minutes, then remove from the pan and drain well.

To precook the noodles, bring a medium pot of water to a boil over medium-high heat. Once boiling, add the noodles and cook for 10 seconds, then quickly drain.

Add the remaining 2 tablespoons (30 ml) of oil to the pan and place over medium heat. Add the noodles and stir to make sure the noodles are not getting lumpy, then add the sauce mixture and stir until the noodles change to a darker color and the sauce is absorbed, 2 minutes. Add the bean sprouts and garlic chives and stir for 30 seconds more. Sprinkle with the peanuts and serve with lime wedges and chile powder.

TIP: Substitute the rice noodles with glass noodles (mung bean noodles) for a good low-carb alternative.

GLUTEN-FREE PAD SEE EEW WITH TOFU

Pad see eew is a Chinese-influenced stir-fried noodle that is commonly served in Thai restaurants. This dish is basically pan-fried rice noodles with your choice of protein and vegetables, usually Chinese broccoli. It is tossed in a nice and dark sweet and sour sauce. You can always add chile pepper powder to bring up the spiciness of this dish. Many Thai people enjoy eating it with peppers pickled in a vinegar sauce. If you can't find fresh or frozen noodles that are ready to cook, buy dried noodles and soak them in room temperature water covered for 1 hour, then drain.

SERVES 4

SEE EEW SAUCE

6 tbsp (90 ml) gluten-free tamari

6 tbsp (83 g) brown sugar

1½ tbsp (23 ml) apple cider vinegar

½ tsp salt

½ tsp ground black pepper

8 tbsp (120 ml) vegetable oil, divided

8 oz (228 g) firm tofu, cut into 1" (2.5-cm) squares

2 tsp (6 g) minced garlic

12 shiitake mushrooms, halved

1 cup (128 g) sliced carrot

20 oz (560 g) flat rice noodles, fresh or frozen

10 stalks Chinese broccoli, cut into 2" (5-cm) lengths

To make the sauce, combine the tamari, brown sugar, apple cider vinegar, salt and black pepper in a small bowl and stir until well combined and the sugar has dissolved.

Heat 6 tablespoons (90 ml) of the oil in a pan over medium heat, add the tofu and fry on each side for 3 minutes, until all the sides are lightly browned, then remove from the pan and drain well.

Add the remaining 2 tablespoons (30 ml) of oil to the pan and place over medium heat. Add the garlic and fry until golden brown, 10 seconds, then add the mushrooms, carrot and rice noodles and stir for 2 minutes to make sure the noodles are not lumping together. Add the sauce, toss well and let it simmer for another 1 to 2 minutes or until the noodles caramelize a little. Add the Chinese broccoli and cook for 30 seconds (if using regular broccoli, cook for 1 minute).

TIP: Serve immediately after cooking for the best taste and texture.

GLUTEN-FREE SPICY NOODLES WITH TEMPEH

(PAD KEE MAO)

Pad Kee Mao, also known as drunken noodles, is a traditional Thai dish cooked with flat rice noodles and mixed vegetables. The name "drunken noodle" came from its popularity with Thai street vendors selling this dish to tipsy party people, as it's a satisfying late-night meal. If you can't find fresh or frozen noodles that are ready to cook, buy dried noodles and soak them in room temperature water covered for 1 hour, then drain.

SERVES 4

SAUCE

2 tbsp (30 ml) gluten-free tamari

2 tbsp (30 ml) gluten-free mushroom stir-fry sauce

2 tbsp (28 g) brown sugar

8 tbsp (120 ml) vegetable oil, divided

8 oz (228 g) tempeh, cut into ½" x 2" (1.3 x 5–cm) sticks

6 Thai chiles, finely chopped

2 tsp (6 g) minced garlic

½ yellow onion, cut into 1" (2.5-cm) squares

½ cup (64 g) sliced carrot

10 button mushrooms, halved

½ red bell pepper, cut into 1" (2.5-cm) squares

½ green bell pepper, cut into 1" (2.5-cm) squares

20 oz (560 g) flat rice noodles, fresh or frozen

2 tbsp (30 ml) vegetable broth

3 green onions, cut into 2" (5-cm) lengths

2 handfuls of Thai sweet basil

To make the sauce, combine the tamari, mushroom stir-fry sauce and brown sugar in a small bowl and mix until well combined and the sugar has dissolved.

Heat 6 tablespoons (90 ml) of the oil in a pan over medium heat, add the tempeh and fry on each side for about 3 minutes or until all the sides are golden brown. Remove from the pan and drain well.

Add the remaining 2 tablespoons (30 ml) of oil to a pan and heat over medium heat, then add the chiles and garlic and fry until golden brown, 10 seconds. Add the yellow onion, carrot, mushrooms, red and green bell peppers, rice noodles and vegetable broth and cook, stirring, until well combined and the vegetables have softened, 2 minutes. Season with the sauce mixture and cook for a few minutes or until the noodles have soaked up the sauce. Add the fried tempeh, green onions and basil and stir for 30 seconds.

Serve immediately after cooking for the best taste and texture.

GLUTEN-FREE SPICY BASIL FRIED RICE WITH TEMPEH

(KAO PAD KRAPRAO)

Thai basil fried rice is one of the most popular and beloved dishes of all time. It is very fast and easy to prepare but still provides great flavor. This dish is basically Gluten-Free Spicy Noodles with Tempeh (page 55) with steamed jasmine rice instead of noodles.

SERVES 4

SAUCE

2½ tbsp (38 ml) gluten-free tamari

2½ tbsp (38 ml) gluten-free mushroom stir-fry sauce

2½ tbsp (34 g) brown sugar

8 tbsp (120 ml) vegetable oil, divided

8 oz (228 g) tempeh, cut into ½" x 2" (1.3 x 5-cm) sticks

4 Thai chiles, finely chopped

1 tsp minced garlic

½ yellow onion, cut into 1" (2.5-cm) squares

2½ cups (435 g) steamed jasmine rice

½ cup (64 g) sliced carrot

8 button mushrooms, halved

½ red bell pepper, cut into 1" (2.5-cm) squares

½ green bell pepper, cut into 1" (2.5-cm) squares

3 green onions, cut into 2" (5-cm) lengths

2 handfuls of Thai sweet basil

1 English cucumber, sliced, for serving

1 lime, cut into wedges, for serving

To make the sauce, combine the tamari, mushroom stir-fry sauce and brown sugar in a small bowl and mix until well combined and the sugar has dissolved.

Heat 6 tablespoons (90 ml) of the oil in a pan over medium heat, add the tempeh and fry on each side for about 3 minutes or until all the sides are golden brown. Remove from the pan and drain well.

Add the remaining 2 tablespoons (30 ml) of oil to a nonstick pan over medium heat, then add the chiles, garlic and yellow onion and fry until golden brown, 10 seconds. Add the steamed rice, carrot, mushrooms and red and green bell peppers and cook, stirring, until well combined and the vegetables have softened. Season with the sauce mixture and cook for about 3 minutes, then add the fried tempeh, green onions and Thai basil and cook for 30 seconds more. Serve with the sliced cucumber and lime wedges on the side.

GLUTEN-FREE GRANDMA FRIED RICE

(KAO PAD KHANA)

Traditional Thai fried rice is always a favorite menu item at most Thai restaurants. This recipe from grandma is your go-to or make-at-home vegan fried rice. The key to making perfect fried rice is using cold leftover rice from your previous meal. What makes Grandma Fried Rice great and different is the special use of the wok; you can smell the burnt flavor of the wok but without any burned food in your dish. Use a wok to bring out the best flavor in this dish, but if you don't have one a nonstick pan will do just fine.

SERVES 4

SAUCE

2½ tbsp (38 ml) gluten-free tamari

2½ tbsp (38 ml) gluten-free mushroom stir-fry sauce

2½ tbsp (34 g) brown sugar

8 tbsp (120 ml) vegetable oil, divided

6 oz (171 g) firm tofu, cut into 1" (2.5-cm) squares

2 tsp (6 g) minced garlic

½ yellow onion, cut into 1" (2.5-cm) squares

2½ cups (435 g) steamed rice

10 grape tomatoes

½ cup (64 g) sliced carrot

8 white mushrooms, halved

8 stalks Chinese broccoli, cut into 2" (5-cm) lengths

1 English cucumber, sliced, for serving

1 lime, cut into wedges, for serving

To make the sauce, combine the tamari, mushroom stir-fry sauce and brown sugar in a small bowl and mix until well combined and the sugar has dissolved.

Heat 6 tablespoons (90 ml) of the oil in a pan over medium heat, add the tofu and fry for about 3 minutes on each side until all the sides are lightly browned. Remove from the pan and drain well.

Add the remaining 2 tablespoons (30 ml) of oil to a wok or nonstick pan over medium heat, add the garlic and yellow onion and fry until golden brown, 10 seconds. Add the steamed rice, tomatoes, carrot and mushrooms and cook, stirring, until well combined and the vegetables have softened, 1 minute. Season with the sauce mixture and stir to make sure the rice is not getting lumpy. Stir for 2 minutes until the sauce soaks into the rice, then add the Chinese broccoli and cook for 30 seconds more (if using regular broccoli, cook for 1 minute). Serve with the sliced cucumber and lime wedges on the side.

GLUTEN-FREE YELLOW CURRY FRIED RICE

(KAO PAD SAPPAROD)

This famous Thai dish of fried rice with pineapple has a lot of sweet and sour flavors from the pineapple and an aromatic fragrance from the yellow curry powder. It is the perfect balance between these two main ingredients that makes a delicious Kao Pad Sapparod.

SERVES 4

SAUCE

2½ tbsp (38 ml) gluten-free tamari

2½ tbsp (38 ml) gluten-free mushroom stir-fry sauce

2½ tbsp (34 g) brown sugar

8 tbsp (120 ml) vegetable oil, divided

6 oz (171 g) firm tofu, cut into 1" (2.5-cm) squares

1 tsp minced garlic

½ yellow onion, cut into 1" (2.5-cm) squares

2½ cups (435 g) steamed rice

1½ tsp (3 g) yellow curry powder

10 grape tomatoes

½ cup (64 g) sliced carrot

8 white mushrooms, halved

1 cup (171 g) sliced pineapple

3 tbsp (24 g) roasted cashews (or peanuts or almonds)

1 English cucumber, sliced, for serving

1 lime, cut into wedges, for serving

To make the sauce, combine the tamari, mushroom stir-fry sauce and brown sugar in a small bowl and mix until well combined and the sugar has dissolved.

Heat 6 tablespoons (90 ml) of the oil in a pan over medium heat, add the tofu and fry for about 3 minutes on each side until all the sides are lightly browned. Remove from the pan and drain well.

Add the remaining 2 tablespoons (30 ml) of oil to a nonstick pan over medium heat, then add the garlic and yellow onion and fry until golden brown, 10 seconds. Add the steamed rice, yellow curry powder, tomatoes, carrot, mushrooms and pineapple and cook, stirring, until well combined and the vegetables have softened, 1 minute. Season with the sauce mixture and stir to make sure the rice is not getting lumpy. Stir for 2 minutes until the sauce soaks into the rice. Garnish with the cashews and serve with the sliced cucumber and lime wedges on the side.

GLUTEN-FREE SALTED BLACK OLIVE FRIED RICE

(KAO PAD NAM LEAB)

This recipe is very different from a typical Thai fried rice. The salted black olives give a unique flavor and smell to the dish. As for the type of salted black olives, I commonly used Chinese black olives for this recipe. This dish is often served with a variety of side items, including fresh cucumber, lime wedges, fresh chiles, roasted cashews, shredded mango and sliced shallot.

SERVES 4

SAUCE

2½ tbsp (38 ml) gluten-free tamari

2½ tbsp (38 ml) gluten-free mushroom stir-fry sauce

2½ tbsp (34 g) brown sugar

8 tbsp (120 ml) vegetable oil, divided

6 oz (171 g) firm tofu, cut into 1" (2.5-cm) squares

2 tsp (6 g) minced garlic

3 cups (522 g) steamed rice

3 tbsp (34 g) roughly chopped salted olives

1 English cucumber, sliced, for serving

1 lime, cut into wedges, for serving

4 tsp (14 g) finely chopped Thai chile, for serving

4 tbsp (32 g) roasted cashews, for serving

4 tbsp (40 g) diced shallot, for serving

1 cup (165 g) sliced green mango or green apple, for serving

To make the sauce, combine the tamari, mushroom stir-fry sauce and brown sugar in a small bowl and mix until well combined and the sugar has dissolved.

Heat 6 tablespoons (90 ml) of the oil in a pan over medium heat, add the tofu and fry for about 3 minutes on each side until all the sides are lightly browned. Remove from the pan and drain well.

Add the remaining 2 tablespoons (30 ml) of oil to a nonstick pan over medium heat, then add the garlic and fry until golden brown, 10 seconds. Add the steamed rice and salted olives and stir until combined. Season with the sauce mixture and stir to make sure the rice is not getting lumpy. Stir for 2 minutes until the sauce soaks into the rice. Serve hot with the crispy tofu, fresh cucumber, lime wedges, chile, roasted cashews, shallot and green mango on the side.

GLUTEN-FREE TOM YUM FRIED RICE

Not many people know that the famous Tom Yum soup can also be cooked as fried rice. The key ingredients are lemongrass, galangal, lime leaves, chile and lime juice. Don't forget the vegan Thai nam prik pao, *or sweet chili paste, without which this dish will not be the same.*

SERVES 4

SAUCE

2½ tbsp (38 ml) gluten-free tamari

2½ tbsp (34 g) brown sugar

2½ tbsp (38 ml) gluten-free mushroom stir-fry sauce

1 tbsp (15 g) Thai Home brand vegan Thai sweet chili paste (nam prik pao)

2 tbsp (30 ml) fresh lime juice

6–8 fresh Thai chiles, finely chopped

2 tbsp (30 ml) vegetable oil

2 tsp (6 g) minced garlic

½ cup (56 g) sliced yellow onion

3 cups (522 g) steamed rice

3 stalks lemongrass, finely sliced

1" (2.5-cm) piece galangal, sliced into thin rounds

8 kaffir lime leaves

10 grape tomatoes

10 white mushrooms, halved

3 green onions, sliced into ¼" (6-mm) rings

3 handfuls of Thai basil

¼ cup (4 g) chopped cilantro

1 English cucumber, sliced, for serving

1 lime, cut into wedges, for serving

To make the sauce, combine the tamari, sugar, mushroom stir-fry sauce, sweet chili paste, lime juice and chiles in a small bowl and stir until well combined and the sugar has dissolved.

Add the vegetable oil to a nonstick pan over medium heat, then add the garlic and yellow onion and fry until golden brown, 10 seconds. Add the steamed rice, lemongrass, galangal, lime leaves, tomatoes and mushrooms and cook, stirring, until well combined and the vegetables have softened, 2 minutes. Season with the sauce and stir to make sure the rice is not getting lumpy. Add the green onions and stir for 1 minute until the sauce soaks into the rice and coats it evenly. Add the basil and stir for 10 seconds more. Sprinkle with the cilantro and serve with the cucumber and lime wedges on the side.

GLUTEN-FREE SUPER BEANS FRIED RICE

This recipe will make your fried rice more interesting by using many of your favorite beans! You can use any kinds of beans that you like. Make sure all the beans are cooked before stir-frying. You can adjust the amount of rice, beans and vegetables as desired as long as they're about the same amount.

SERVES 4

SAUCE

2½ tbsp (38 ml) gluten-free tamari

2½ tbsp (38 ml) gluten-free mushroom stir-fry sauce

2½ tbsp (34 g) brown sugar

8 tbsp (120 ml) vegetable oil, divided

6 oz (171 g) firm tofu, cut into 1" (2.5-cm) squares

2 tsp (6 g) minced garlic

½ yellow onion, cut into 1" (2.5-cm) squares

3 cups (522 g) steamed rice

10 grape tomatoes

¼ cup (32 g) diced carrot

¼ cup (48 g) cooked red beans

¼ cup (48 g) cooked edamame

¼ cup (48 g) cooked chickpeas

¼ cup (40 g) sweet corn

2 cups (142 g) chopped broccoli

1 English cucumber, sliced, for serving

1 lime, cut into wedges, for serving

To make the sauce, combine the tamari, mushroom stir-fry sauce and brown sugar in a small bowl and mix until well combined and the sugar has dissolved.

Heat 6 tablespoons (90 ml) of the oil in a pan over medium heat, add the tofu and fry for 3 minutes on each side until all sides are lightly browned. Remove from the pan and drain well.

Add the remaining 2 tablespoons (30 ml) of oil to a nonstick pan over medium heat, then add the garlic and yellow onion and fry until golden brown, 10 seconds. Add the steamed rice, tomatoes, carrot, red beans, edamame, chickpeas, sweet corn and broccoli and cook, stirring, until combined and the vegetables have softened, 2 minutes. Season with the sauce mixture and stir to make sure the rice is not getting lumpy. Stir for a few minutes until the sauce soaks into the rice. Serve with the sliced cucumber and lime wedges on the side.

EASY STARTERS

Starters, or snacks that we eat before the main meal, have become some of our favorite dishes. I want to introduce you to popular Thai starters that are quick and simple and contain only a few ingredients. The instructions are easy to understand even for the beginner Thai cook and require less than 15 minutes of your time. These starters are so delicious that you'll want to make a whole meal of them and skip the main dishes.

SON-IN-LAW TOFU

(TAO HOO LOOK KUEY)

In this starter, we fry tofu until it's yellow and crispy on the outside but still soft inside. It is then topped with a sweet and sour tamarind sauce. The original recipe is made with eggs, but I substitute tofu. I promise you will not be disappointed!

SERVES 4

1 cup plus 1 tbsp (255 ml) vegetable oil, divided, plus more as needed

2 shallots, very thinly sliced

21 oz (595 g) firm tofu, cut into 1" (2.5-cm) squares

10 dried Thai chiles

½ cup (100 g) palm sugar

½ cup (120 ml) tamarind juice

½ cup (120 ml) thin soy sauce

½ cup (8 g) chopped cilantro

Heat 1 cup (240 ml) of the oil in a pan over medium-high heat. Add the shallots and fry until lightly browned, 10 minutes, then remove from the pan immediately and drain well. Pat the tofu dry with a paper towel and cut it into bite-size cubes. Fry the tofu in the oil left after frying the shallots, adding more oil if needed, for 3 minutes on all sides until they turn a crispy golden brown but are still soft on the inside. Remove from the pan and drain well. Next, fry the dried chiles for about 30 seconds, remove from the pan, drain and set aside.

Add the remaining 1 tablespoon (15 ml) of oil to a dry, clean pan over medium heat, then add the palm sugar, tamarind juice and soy sauce and cook, stirring, until the sugar melts. Then cook for 1 minute longer until you have a rich and sticky sauce. Remove the pan from the heat. Add the crispy tofu to the sauce and mix until the tofu is coated well. Top with the fried shallots, fried chiles and cilantro.

Serve immediately after cooking with steamed rice, while the tofu is still crispy, for the best taste!

CRISPY TOFU DIPPED IN SWEET AND SOUR SAUCE

Crispy fried tofu, or Tao Hoo Tod in Thailand, is a popular street snack that can be eaten any time of the year, including during the vegan festival. Serve it with the delicious sweet and sour peanut-tamarind sauce for dipping perfection.

SERVES 4

3 cups (720 ml) vegetable oil

21 oz (595 g) firm tofu, cut into 1" (2.5-cm) squares

SWEET AND SOUR SAUCE

1 cup (200 g) sugar

½ cup (120 ml) water

½ cup (120 ml) apple cider vinegar

1 tbsp (15 ml) tamari

1 tbsp (18 g) salt

2 tbsp (30 ml) chili garlic sauce

1 tbsp (9 g) crushed roasted peanuts

Heat the oil in a pan over medium heat to 350°F (180°C), and fry the tofu for about 3 minutes or until golden brown on each side and cooked through. Remove from the pan and drain well.

To make the sweet and sour sauce, combine the sugar, water, apple cider vinegar, tamari, salt and chili garlic sauce in a saucepan over medium heat and stir until the sugar dissolves, then simmer for 2 to 3 minutes or until the sauce is thick. Serve the tofu with the sauce for dipping. Sprinkle the dipping sauce with the peanuts.

SPICY CRISPY SWEET CORN PATTIES

(TOD MUN KHAO POD)

The original recipe these corn patties are based on is tod mun pla, *which is fish curry cake patties. Spicy Crispy Sweet Corn Patties, or Tod Mun Khao Pod, is an easy snack to make and sweet corn is a good source of carbohydrates that can give you some energy when yours is lacking in the afternoon.*

SERVES 4

CUCUMBER SALAD

¼ cup (60 ml) water

1 cup (220 g) brown sugar

¼ cup (60 ml) apple cider vinegar

1 tsp salt

1 English cucumber, cut into 1" (2.5-cm) squares

½ tsp chopped shallot

2 Thai chiles, finely chopped

2 tbsp (16 g) crushed roasted peanuts, for topping

CORN PATTIES

4 cups (577 g) sweet corn kernels

6 tbsp (48 g) cornstarch

1 tbsp (15 g) Thai Home brand vegan Thai red curry paste

2 tbsp (16 g) shredded kaffir lime leaves

6 tbsp (90 ml) water

3 cups (720 ml) vegetable oil

To make the cucumber salad, combine the water, sugar, apple cider vinegar and salt in a saucepan and cook over medium heat, stirring, until the sugar and salt have dissolved. Remove from the heat and let cool. Once cool, add the cucumber, shallot and Thai chiles, and marinate for 15 to 20 minutes, then drain.

To make the corn patties, in a mixing bowl, combine the sweet corn, cornstarch, red curry paste, lime leaves and water, tossing well until combined. Heat the oil in a pan over medium heat to 350°F (180°C), drop 1 tablespoon (15 g) of the corn mixture at a time into the oil and fry for about 6 minutes or until golden brown on each side and cooked through. Remove from the pan and drain well. Place the crispy patties on a plate, and serve with the peanuts and cucumber salad.

TIPS: If you don't like spicy food, decrease the amount of curry paste to your taste.

Flatten the patties before frying to make them cook faster.

ENOKI MUSHROOM FRITTERS

Mushrooms are the new meat! In this recipe, enoki mushrooms are battered and deep-fried until they're golden and crispy. These fritters could be served as snacks or starters before the main course, and they are very addictive!

SERVES 4

HOT SAUCE

2 tbsp (30 ml) apple cider vinegar

3 tbsp (38 g) sugar

3 tbsp (45 ml) sriracha sauce

1 tbsp (15 ml) tamari

FRITTERS

¼ cup (32 g) cornstarch

1 tsp pepper

½ tsp salt

1 tbsp (15 ml) tamari

½ cup (120 ml) water

3 cups (720 ml) vegetable oil

21 oz (600 g) enoki mushrooms, cleaned, roots trimmed and separated into small bunches

To make the hot sauce, combine the apple cider vinegar, sugar, sriracha and tamari in a small bowl and mix until the sugar has dissolved.

To make the fritters, combine the cornstarch, pepper, salt, tamari and water in a medium bowl and mix well. Heat the oil in a pan over medium heat to 350°F (180°C). Add the enoki mushroom bunches to the batter and toss until well coated. Drop the coated enoki bunches into the oil and fry for about 4 minutes or until golden brown on each side and cooked through. Remove from the pan and drain well. Place the fritters on a plate and serve with the hot sauce.

TIP: While frying, keep separating the enoki mushroom bunches so they don't stick together.

GOLDEN CRISPY TARO

Taro is a tropical root vegetable used widely in Southeast Asia for savory dishes and desserts. The natural sugars from taro give a sweet and nutty flavor, and it is perfectly balanced when served with a sweet and sour peanut sauce. This recipe will transform taro into a whole new experience. You can also try this recipe with different kinds of vegetables, such as kabocha squash, carrot, sweet potato and green papaya.

SERVES 4

SWEET AND SOUR SAUCE

1 cup (200 g) sugar

½ cup (120 ml) water

½ cup (120 ml) apple cider vinegar

1 tbsp (15 ml) tamari

1 tbsp (18 g) salt

2 tbsp (30 ml) chili garlic sauce

3 tbsp (27 g) crushed roasted peanuts (for topping)

5 cups (750 g) shredded taro

6 tbsp (48 g) cornstarch

1 tsp salt

1 tsp yellow curry powder

½ cup (120 ml) water

1 tbsp (15 ml) tamari

3 cups (720 ml) vegetable oil

To make the sweet and sour sauce, combine the sugar, water, apple cider vinegar, tamari, salt and chili garlic sauce in a saucepan over medium heat and cook, stirring, until the sugar has dissolved, then simmer for 2 to 3 minutes or until the sauce is thick.

In a mixing bowl, combine the shredded taro, cornstarch, salt, yellow curry powder, water and tamari and toss well until combined. Heat the oil in a pan over medium heat to 350°F (180°C), drop 1 tablespoon (15 g) of the taro mixture at a time into the oil and fry for about 6 minutes or until golden brown on each side and cooked through. Remove from the pan and drain well. Place the crispy taro on a plate, and sprinkle the peanuts on the sweet and sour sauce before serving.

TIP: If you prefer a spicy sauce, add ½ teaspoon of ground chile powder to the sweet and sour sauce.

SUGAR SNAP PEAS

This dish is a traditional Thai recipe that is popular for its rich flavors. This is another type of Thai curry that does not require the use of coconut milk. Serve with steamed white jasmine rice for a full meal.

(PAD PRIK KHING)

SERVES 4

PRIK KHING SAUCE

2 tbsp (30 ml) tamari

2 tbsp (28 g) brown sugar

2 tbsp (30 ml) vegetable oil

1 tbsp (15 g) vegan Thai red curry paste

6 cups (378 g) sugar snap peas

1 tbsp (8 g) finely sliced kaffir lime leaves

1 tbsp (14 g) finely sliced ginger

To make the sauce, combine the tamari, brown sugar, vegetable oil and vegan Thai red curry paste in a small bowl and mix until well combined and the sugar has dissolved.

Add the sauce mixture to a pan over medium heat, then add the sugar snap peas, kaffir lime leaves and ginger and sauté for 30 seconds. Serve hot as an appetizer or with steamed rice for a meal.

THAI-STYLE ASPARAGUS

This is a delicious, simple, quick and easy asparagus dish to eat alongside other spicy food or on its own. You can also substitute the asparagus with any other vegetables you like.

SERVES 4

SAUCE

2 tbsp (30 ml) tamari

2 tbsp (30 ml) mushroom stir-fry sauce

2 tsp (9 g) brown sugar

2 lb (908 g) asparagus, ends snapped off

1 tbsp (15 ml) vegetable oil

2 tbsp (6 g) minced garlic

4 Thai chiles, chopped

1 tbsp (15 ml) vegetable broth

To make the sauce, combine the tamari, mushroom stir-fry sauce and brown sugar in a small bowl and mix until well combined and the sugar has dissolved.

Bring a pot of water to a boil over medium-high heat, add the asparagus and cook for 6 to 8 minutes or until it is as tender as you like. Remove from the pan and drain well. Place the cooked asparagus on a serving plate.

Heat the vegetable oil in a pan over medium heat, add the garlic and fry until golden brown, about 10 seconds, then add the sauce mixture, chiles and vegetable broth and cook, stirring, until the sauce thickens, about 1 minute. Pour the sauce over the cooked asparagus and serve hot.

CRISPY CURRY SOY CURLS

These crispy soy curls can be eaten as a snack or used as a side dish. The combination of aromatic herbs and spices from the red curry paste blend together well and form a delicious crispy vegan snack that is perfect for movie time.

SERVES 4

PRIK KHING SAUCE

2 tbsp (30 ml) tamari

2 tbsp (28 g) brown sugar

2 tbsp (30 ml) vegetable oil

1 tbsp (15 g) vegan Thai red curry paste

3 cups (120 g) soy curls

½ cup (120 ml) vegetable oil

3 tbsp (24 g) finely sliced kaffir lime leaves

1 tbsp (14 g) finely sliced ginger

To make the sauce, combine the tamari, brown sugar, vegetable oil and vegan Thai red curry paste in a small bowl and mix until well combined and the sugar has dissolved.

Soak the soy curls in water to soften per the package directions, drain well and let dry.

Heat the oil in a deep pan over medium heat, add the soy curls and fry until they turn crispy and golden brown, 10 minutes. Drain well and let cool.

Add the sauce mixture to a separate pan over medium heat, then add the crispy soy curls, lime leaves and ginger and toss until everything is coated in the sauce. Serve at room temperature with rice, if desired.

GARLIC AND PEPPER HON-SHIMEJI MUSHROOMS

This simple but delicious mushroom dish will make your dinner more interesting. This dish can be eaten on its own or served alongside other spicy foods.

SERVES 4

SAUCE

2 tbsp (30 ml) tamari

2 tbsp (30 ml) mushroom stir-fry sauce

2 tsp (9 g) brown sugar

1 tsp ground black pepper

¼ cup (60 ml) vegetable oil

4 tbsp (32 g) minced garlic

6 cups (420 g) hon-shimeji mushrooms

1 tbsp (15 ml) vegetable broth

To make the sauce, combine the tamari, mushroom stir-fry sauce, brown sugar and black pepper in a small bowl and mix until well combined and the sugar has dissolved.

Heat the vegetable oil in a pan over medium heat, add the garlic and fry until golden brown, 10 seconds, then add the mushrooms, sauce mixture and vegetable broth, and cook, stirring, for 3 to 4 minutes.

FRESH VEGGIE ROLLS

Fresh veggie rolls are inspired by the Thai-Vietnamese people who live in the northeastern region of Thailand. The original dish is called bo bia sot, *and it normally contains pork loaf, mint leaf, green leaf lettuce, rice noodles, bean sprouts and carrot. You can add your favorite leafy greens as well. These fresh veggie rolls are incredibly easy to prepare and a healthier appetizer option before the main course. This dish is perfect for summertime; pair them with peanut sauce and you will never want to stop eating them!*

MAKES 8 ROLLS

PEANUT DRESSING

½ cup (130 g) peanut butter

1 cup (220 g) brown sugar

½ cup (120 ml) water

½ cup (120 ml) apple cider vinegar

1 tbsp (15 ml) tamari

1 tbsp (18 g) salt

2 tbsp (30 ml) chili garlic sauce

1 tbsp (8 g) crushed roasted peanuts, for topping

VEGGIE ROLLS

8 spring roll rice paper wrappers (size 28)

1 avocado, peeled, pitted and cut into 8 equal pieces

3 cups (141 g) chopped romaine lettuce

2 cups (220 g) shredded carrot

2 cups (140 g) shredded purple cabbage

1 seedless cucumber, cut into ½" x 3" (2 x 8-cm) sticks

1 cup (26 g) mint leaves

To make the peanut dressing, combine the peanut butter, brown sugar, water, apple cider vinegar, tamari, salt and chili garlic sauce in a saucepan over medium heat and cook, stirring, until the sugar has dissolved, then simmer for 2 to 3 minutes or until the sauce is thick.

To make the veggie rolls, fill a big bowl with warm water, dip a wrapper in the water for a quick 3 seconds to soften it, then lay it on a flat plate. Place one piece of avocado, romaine, carrot, cabbage, cucumber and mint leaves on one end of the wrapper. Fold the roll halfway, fold both ends inward, then roll to the end. Make sure all the fillings remain tight and stay inside the roll. Repeat with the remaining ingredients.

Sprinkle the peanuts on top of the sauce and serve with the rolls.

SWIMMING RAMA WITH PEANUT DRESSING

(RAM LONG SONG)

This is one of the most popular dishes in Thai restaurants. It is a single dish consisting of meat and steamed vegetables tossed in peanut dressing with rice served on the side. The traditional version uses steamed Chinese broccoli as its main vegetable. However, Chinese broccoli has a unique aroma and bitter flavor that many people do not enjoy. In this recipe, we use regular broccoli and carrot as the main vegetables, but you can use your favorite veggies if you prefer. I recommend string beans, spinach or kale. Serve with steamed rice or steamed rice noodles.

SERVES 4

PEANUT DRESSING

½ cup (130 g) peanut butter

1 cup (220 g) brown sugar

½ cup (120 ml) water

½ cup (120 ml) apple cider vinegar

1 tbsp (15 ml) tamari

1 tbsp (18 g) salt

2 tbsp (30 ml) chili garlic sauce

8 oz (228 g) fresh tofu, cut into 1" (2.5-cm) squares

8 cups (560 g) chopped broccoli

1½ cups (165 g) shredded carrot

2 Thai chiles, finely chopped

3 tbsp (27 g) crushed roasted peanuts

To make the peanut dressing, combine the peanut butter, brown sugar, water, apple cider vinegar, tamari, salt and chili garlic sauce in a saucepan over medium heat and cook, stirring, until the sugar has dissolved, then simmer for 2 to 3 minutes or until the sauce is thick.

Prepare a large bowl of ice water. Bring a pot of water to a boil over medium-high heat, add the tofu and cook for 30 to 45 seconds. Remove from the water with a strainer and transfer to a plate to cool. Return the water to a boil, add the broccoli and cook for 1 minute, then quickly transfer to the bowl of ice water to stop the cooking, then drain well.

Place the steamed broccoli on a plate, top with the shredded carrot and steamed tofu, drizzle with the peanut dressing and sprinkle with the chile and peanuts.

TOFU SATAY

This delicious Indonesian- or Malaysian-inspired tofu is marinated in tamari with yellow curry powder. It is always served with peanut sauce and pickled cucumber. Most people eat it as a snack, but it can be eaten as a meal with steamed jasmine rice or a slice of toasted bread. Satay is traditionally prepared on a charcoal grill, but for simplicity we will pan-fry the tofu in this recipe. It is the perfect choice for snacking or a summer cookout party. For a change of pace, substitute the tofu for soy curls or zucchini! Serve with toasted whole wheat bread to soak up the sauce.

MAKES 6 TO 8 SKEWERS

PEANUT DRESSING

½ cup (130 g) 100% natural peanut butter

1 cup (220 g) brown sugar

½ cup (120 ml) water

½ cup (120 ml) apple cider vinegar

1 tbsp (15 ml) tamari

1 tbsp (18 g) salt

2 tbsp (30 ml) chili garlic sauce

CUCUMBER SALAD

½ cup (120 ml) water

1 cup (220 g) brown sugar

¼ cup (60 ml) apple cider vinegar

½ tsp salt

1 English cucumber, cut into 1" (2.5-cm) squares

½ tsp chopped shallot

1 Thai chile, finely chopped

TOFU

2 tbsp (30 ml) tamari

2 tbsp (16 g) yellow curry powder

14 oz (400 g) firm tofu, cut into 4" x ¾" (10 x 2–cm) sticks

3 tbsp (45 ml) vegetable oil

3 tbsp (45 ml) coconut cream

To make the peanut dressing, combine the peanut butter, brown sugar, water, apple cider vinegar, tamari, salt and chili garlic sauce in a saucepan over medium heat and cook, stirring, until the sugar has dissolved, then simmer for 2 to 3 minutes or until the sauce is thick.

To make the cucumber salad, combine the water, sugar, apple cider vinegar and salt in a saucepan and heat until the sugar and salt have dissolved, then remove from the heat and let cool. Once cool, add the cucumber, shallot and Thai chile and marinate for 15 to 20 minutes, then drain.

To make the tofu, combine the tamari and curry powder in a wide bowl, add the tofu, stir to coat, then let marinate for 10 minutes. Remove from the marinade and thread onto 6 to 8 bamboo skewers.

Heat the oil in a pan over medium heat and fry the tofu on each side until golden brown, about 3 minutes per side, then add the coconut cream and let it simmer with the tofu for 1 minute. Serve with the peanut sauce for dipping and the cucumber salad on the side.

TIP: Use a charcoal grill for perfect authentic tofu satay. Prepare the grill to high heat, about 400°F (204°C). Place the satay on the grill and cook 2 to 3 minutres per side, or until cooked through.

15-MINUTE SALADS AND SOUPS

Yum, the Thai word for "mix" or "salad," is a popular menu item for many people. Thai salads have delicious flavors and the fragrant aroma of fresh herbs. I want to introduce you to a variety of Thai salads, including authentic and fusion Thai recipes. Spicy, sweet and sour are the three key flavors to make your favorite *yum*, well, yummy. Our three most popular Thai soups are in this chapter as well.

For centuries, rice has been the main food for Thai people, whether it is regular rice or sticky rice. At the Thai dinner table, everybody shares the main courses, or what we call *kub khao*, and we always consume *kub khao* with rice. With their intense aromatics and flavor, Thai soups and salads are considered *kub khao* as well, and many of them pair well with rice, stir-fries, curries and noodles.

THREE FLAVORS TOFU SALAD

(TAO HOO MA NAW)

The main ingredients in this salad are lime, garlic, fresh chiles and your protein of choice. In this recipe, we are going to use tofu as the protein, but soy curls, tempeh or veggie meat are good options as well. This dish is super tasty, healthy and light, yet completely filling at the same time. You can eat it as is or serve it over rice or steamed vegetables.

SERVES 4

DRESSING

8 Thai chiles, finely chopped

4 tbsp (32 g) minced garlic

½ cup (110 g) brown sugar

4 tbsp (60 ml) lime juice

4 tbsp (60 ml) tamari

1 tbsp (15 ml) apple cider vinegar

1 tsp salt

SALAD

¼ cup (60 ml) vegetable oil

8 oz (228 g) firm tofu, cut into 1" (2.5-cm) squares

6 tbsp (60 g) sliced shallot

4 cups (220 g) organic spring salad mix

Mint leaves, for garnish

To make the dressing, combine the chiles, garlic, sugar, lime juice, tamari, apple cider vinegar and salt in a small bowl and stir until the sugar has dissolved.

To make the salad, heat the oil in a pan over medium heat, add the tofu and fry on each side for about 3 minutes or until all the sides are lightly browned, then remove from the pan and drain well. Add the shallot to the oil and fry until crispy and golden, about 10 minutes.

Make a bed of salad greens on a plate. Top with the tofu and shallot and drizzle with the dressing. Garnish the salad with mint.

EGGPLANT SALAD

(YUM MA KHEAU YAW)

Many people don't know how to cook eggplant properly, but this dish will teach you how. This is my favorite way of cooking eggplant because it is spicy, sweet and sour and makes a quick and delicious healthy meal.

SERVES 4

DRESSING

6 Thai chiles, finely chopped

1½ tbsp (12 g) minced garlic

¼ cup (55 g) brown sugar

2 tbsp (30 ml) lime juice

3 tbsp (45 ml) tamari

½ tbsp (8 ml) apple cider vinegar

½ tsp salt

1 tbsp (15 g) vegan Thai sweet chili paste (nam prik pao)

SALAD

3 tbsp (45 ml) vegetable oil, plus more if needed

1 cup (150 g) crumbled firm tofu

2 Chinese eggplant, sliced into ½" (1.3-cm)-thick rounds

4 tbsp (40 g) sliced shallot

2 tbsp (20 g) finely sliced red onion

2 tbsp (12 g) finely sliced green onion

½ cup (8 g) chopped cilantro

3 cups (165 g) spring salad mix

1 cup (96 g) chopped mint leaves

To make the dressing, combine the chiles, garlic, sugar, lime juice, tamari, apple cider vinegar, salt and chili paste in a small bowl and stir until the sugar has dissolved.

To make the salad, heat the oil in a pan over medium heat, add the crumbled tofu and cook, stirring, until golden brown, 5 to 8 minutes, then remove from the pan and drain well. Use the same oil to pan-fry the eggplant on each side for 3 minutes until both sides are golden brown, adding more oil if needed, then remove from the pan and drain well. Let cool. Finally, add the shallot to the oil and fry until crispy and golden, 10 minutes. Remove from the pan and drain well.

In a large bowl, combine the fried eggplant, red onion, green onion, cilantro, half of the fried tofu and the dressing. Mix until well combined. Make a bed of salad greens on a plate. Top with the eggplant mixture, fried shallot, remaining fried tofu and mint leaves.

TIP: Pair this salad with one of the curry dishes to balance the fresh and light salad with the rich and creamy curry.

POMELO SALAD

(YUM SOM OH)

Pomelo, also known as shaddock, Bali lemon or Chinese grapefruit, has a slightly bitter, tangy and sweet flavor, making it a perfect fruit salad item. Pomelo can be found at most Asian grocery stores, but if you can't find one near you, red grapefruit or blood oranges would be great as well. A bright citrus dressing balances the tangy, salty and sweet, and roasted coconut chips, fried garlic and roasted peanuts add a crunchy texture. For the best taste and texture, serve and eat immediately, while all the flavors and textures are still fresh.

SERVES 4

DRESSING

1 tsp ground chile powder

2 tbsp (16 g) fried garlic

½ cup (110 g) brown sugar

4 tbsp (60 ml) lime juice

4 tbsp (60 ml) tamari

1 tbsp (15 ml) apple cider vinegar

1 tsp salt

SALAD

1 small pomelo

8 tbsp (72 g) roasted peanuts or cashews

8 tbsp (43 g) roasted coconut flakes

6 kaffir lime leaves, finely chopped (optional)

4 cups (220 g) spring salad mix

8 tbsp (80 g) fried shallot

½ cup (13 g) sliced mint leaves

To make the dressing, combine the chile powder, garlic, sugar, lime juice, tamari, apple cider vinegar and salt in a small bowl and stir until the sugar has dissolved.

To make the salad, peel the pomelo, divide into segments and carefully remove the bitter white membrane from each segment. Be gentle so you don't burst the juice sacs and end up with a watery salad. Place the pomelo segments, peanuts, coconut flakes and lime leaves, if using, in a mixing bowl, add the dressing and toss gently to combine. Make a bed of greens on a plate, top with the pomelo mixture and garnish with the fried shallot and mint.

TIP: Chill the peeled pomelo in the fridge to make the salad taste more refreshing!

BANANA BLOSSOM SALAD

You might not know that banana blossoms are edible! The flavor ranges from subtle to strongly astringent. The inner light-yellow part is the most popular for cooking. Banana blossom, or hue plee, *is a popular ingredient in Thai cuisine. We use it in stir-fries, soups, salads and curries and even eat it as a vegetable side dish. You can find fresh or canned banana blossoms at Asian grocery stores. Try this unique salad—banana blossoms might become your new favorite ingredient!*

SERVES 4

DRESSING

1 tsp ground chile powder

1½ tbsp (12 g) minced garlic

¼ cup (55 g) brown sugar

2 tbsp (30 ml) lime juice

3 tbsp (45 ml) tamari

½ tbsp (8 ml) apple cider vinegar

½ tsp salt

1 tbsp (15 g) vegan Thai sweet chili paste (nam prik pao)

SALAD

1 tbsp (15 ml) vegetable oil

1 tsp bean paste (can be substituted with ¼ tsp salt)

8 button mushrooms, halved

4 cups (400 g) thinly sliced young banana blossoms (if you can't find fresh, substitute canned)

½ cup (120 ml) water

8 tbsp (43 g) roasted coconut flakes

8 tbsp (72 g) roasted peanuts or cashews

1 cup (16 g) chopped cilantro

4 tbsp (40 g) finely sliced red onion

4 tbsp (24 g) finely sliced green onion

4 kaffir lime leaves, finely chopped (optional)

3 cups (165 g) spring salad mix

8 tbsp (80 g) fried shallot

½ cup (13 g) sliced mint leaves

To make the dressing, combine the chile powder, garlic, sugar, lime juice, tamari, apple cider vinegar, salt and chili paste in a small bowl and stir until the sugar has dissolved.

To make the salad, heat the oil in a pan over high heat, add the bean paste, mushrooms, banana blossoms and water and cook for 1 minute or until the vegetables are softened and the water has dried up; transfer to a mixing bowl. Add the coconut flakes, peanuts, cilantro, red onion, green onion, lime leaves, if using, and the dressing and toss until well combined. Make a bed of greens on a plate, top with the salad mixture and garnish with the fried shallot and mint.

SWEET CORN SALAD

This simple and delicious corn salad is so refreshing. I like to buy fresh corn and boil or steam it, then cut the kernels off the cobs in strips as deep as possible. The traditional way of making this salad is with a mortar and pestle to first grind the garlic and chile into a paste, then add the sugar, salt and tamari and mix them together.

SERVES 4

DRESSING

4 Thai chiles, finely chopped

1 tbsp (8 g) minced garlic

3 tbsp (45 ml) melted palm sugar

4 tbsp (60 ml) lime juice

3 tbsp (45 ml) tamari

½ tsp salt

SALAD

3 cups (450 g) sweet corn

1 cup (110 g) shredded carrot

1 cup (72 g) shredded red cabbage

8 green beans, cut into 2" (5-cm) lengths

10 grape tomatoes, halved

3 cups (165 g) spring salad mix

To make the dressing, combine the chiles, garlic, palm sugar, lime juice, tamari and salt in a small bowl and stir until the sugar has dissolved.

To make the salad, add the corn, carrot, cabbage, green beans, grape tomatoes and dressing to a mixing bowl. Toss the mixture well until the juice comes out of the tomatoes. Make a bed of greens on a plate and spoon the corn salad on top.

TIP: Add crushed cashews or peanuts for a textural contrast.

GLASS NOODLE SALAD

(YUM WOONSEN)

Vermicelli or mung bean noodles are commonly used in the Thai and Asian kitchen. The noodles are white and very thin and, once they are cooked and become transparent, have a chewy texture. In Thai cuisine, we use glass noodles in stir-fries, soups, curries and salads. Glass noodles are a good substitute if you want to create a low-carb noodle dish.

SERVES 4

DRESSING

6 Thai chiles, finely chopped

1½ tbsp (12 g) minced garlic

¼ cup (55 g) brown sugar

2 tbsp (30 ml) lime juice

3 tbsp (45 ml) tamari

½ tbsp (8 ml) apple cider vinegar

½ tsp salt

1 tbsp (15 g) Thai Home brand vegan Thai sweet chili paste (nam prik pao)

SALAD

10 oz (280 g) Thai mung bean noodles

6 tbsp (90 ml) vegetable oil

4 oz (114 g) firm tofu, cut into ½" (1.3-cm) squares

3 cups (720 ml) water

3 tbsp (30 g) finely sliced red onion

3 tbsp (18 g) finely sliced green onion

2 Chinese celery stalks, cut into ¾" (2-cm) lengths, leaves chopped

8 grape tomatoes, halved

1 cup (16 g) chopped cilantro

2 cups (110 g) spring salad mix

½ cup (13 g) chopped mint leaves

3 tbsp (27 g) whole roasted peanuts

3 tbsp (24 g) whole roasted cashews

To make the dressing, combine the chiles, garlic, sugar, lime juice, tamari, apple cider vinegar, salt and chili paste in a small bowl and stir until the sugar has dissolved.

To make the salad, soak the noodles in cold water for about 10 minutes, drain and cut into 6-inch (15-cm) lengths.

Heat the oil in a pan over medium heat, add the tofu and fry for 3 minutes on each side until all the sides are lightly browned, then remove from the pan and drain well.

Prepare a bowl of ice water. Add the 3 cups (720 ml) of water to a small pot and bring to a boil over medium-high heat. Add the mung bean noodles and cook for 15 seconds, then immediately transfer to the cold water to cool; drain well.

Add the fried tofu, red onion, green onion, celery, grape tomatoes, cilantro, cooked noodles and dressing to a mixing bowl. Toss the mixture well until the juice comes out of the tomatoes. Make a bed of salad greens on a plate and spoon the salad mixture on top. Garnish with the mint leaves, peanuts and cashews.

TEMPEH LEMONGRASS SALAD

If you have ever been to a Thai village, you will see lemongrass growing in almost every herb garden. Many Thai people like to grow their own cooking herbs, such as mint, lemongrass, basil, galangal and many more. Lemongrass is an herb with an aromatic lemony scent. Fresh lemongrass is preferred for cooking, as it has better texture and flavor. We only use a certain part of the lemongrass stalk—the yellow section—as it is the youngest part. Lemongrass is fibrous, so be sure to cut and slice it very thinly before adding it to your salad. For this salad, we use tempeh, but feel free to switch it up with tofu, soy curls or veggie meat. This light, healthy and refreshing salad is perfect for the warm summer months.

SERVES 4

DRESSING

1 tsp ground chile powder

1½ tbsp (12 g) minced garlic

¼ cup (55 g) brown sugar

2 tbsp (30 ml) lime juice

3 tbsp (45 ml) tamari

½ tbsp (8 ml) apple cider vinegar

½ tsp salt

1 tbsp (15 g) vegan Thai sweet chili paste (nam prik pao)

SALAD

6 tbsp (90 ml) vegetable oil

8 oz (228 g) tempeh, cut into ½" x 2" (1.3 x 5–cm) sticks

8 tbsp (38 g) finely sliced lemongrass

4 tbsp (32 g) finely sliced kaffir lime leaves

6 tbsp (60 g) finely sliced shallot

1 cup (26 g) chopped mint leaves

1 cup (16 g) chopped cilantro

8 grape tomatoes, halved

2 cups (110 g) spring salad mix

To make the dressing, combine the chile powder, garlic, sugar, lime juice, tamari, apple cider vinegar, salt and chili paste in a small bowl and stir until the sugar has dissolved.

To make the salad, heat the oil in a pan over medium heat, add the tempeh and fry for 3 minutes on each side until all the sides are lightly browned, then remove from the pan and drain well.

Place the crispy tempeh, lemongrass, lime leaves, shallot, mint leaves, cilantro, tomatoes and dressing in a mixing bowl. Toss the mixture well until the juice comes out of the tomatoes. Make a bed of greens on a plate and spoon the salad mixture on top.

GREEN PAPAYA SALAD

(SOM TUM)

Papaya salad, or Som Tum, is an iconic dish in Thailand, and you can find it at almost any street stall. It has a perfect balance of sour, spicy, salty, sweet and savory flavors. Thai people eat it as a snack or as a meal with sticky rice. For a better crunch and a fresh nutty aroma, I recommend roasting the peanuts in your kitchen.

SERVES 4

DRESSING

4 Thai chiles, finely chopped

1 tbsp (8 g) minced garlic

3 tbsp (45 ml) melted palm sugar

4 tbsp (60 ml) lime juice

3 tbsp (45 ml) tamari

½ tsp salt

SALAD

13 oz (364 g) shredded green papaya

1 cup (110 g) shredded carrot

7 green beans, cut into 2" (5-cm) lengths

10 grape tomatoes, halved

3 tbsp (27 g) crushed roasted peanuts

2 cups (110 g) spring salad mix

2 tbsp (18 g) whole peanuts

To make the dressing, combine the chiles, garlic, palm sugar, lime juice, tamari and salt in a small bowl and stir until the sugar has dissolved.

To make the salad, add the green papaya, carrot, green beans, grape tomatoes, crushed peanuts and salad dressing to a mixing bowl. Toss the mixture well until the juice comes out of the tomatoes. Make a bed of greens on a plate and spoon the salad mixture on top. Garnish with the whole peanuts.

TIP: If you have a mortar and pestle, pound the chiles and garlic until fine, then add the palm sugar and mash until dissolved. Add the green beans and pound until broken, then add the tomatoes and mash until the juice comes out. Add the tamari, lime juice and salt and stir until mixed well, then add the green papaya and toss to combine.

GREEN MANGO SALAD ON CRISPY TEMPEH

My favorite memory of mango salad is of a school summer break, when my friends and I climbed the mango tree of a neighbor, grabbed a few green mangoes, made mango salad and ate it at my friend's house. That day I learned that to make this dish taste good, you must look for crisp, green mangoes, to provide the sourness and crunchy texture for your salad. This salad is bursting with tropical flavors—fruity, spicy, sweet and sour—and is the perfect foil for crispy tempeh.

SERVES 4

DRESSING

1 tsp ground chile powder

¼ cup (55 g) brown sugar

2 tbsp (30 ml) lime juice

3 tbsp (45 ml) tamari

½ tsp salt

1 tbsp (15 g) Thai Home brand vegan Thai sweet chili paste (nam prik pao)

SALAD

6 tbsp (90 ml) vegetable oil

8 oz (228 g) tempeh, cut into ½" x 2" (1.3 x 5-cm) sticks

3 cups (495 g) shredded green mango

1 cup (110 g) shredded carrot

4 tbsp (36 g) whole roasted peanuts or cashews

3 tbsp (30 g) finely sliced red onion

3 tbsp (18 g) finely sliced green onion

2 cups (110 g) spring salad mix

4 tbsp (19 g) roasted coconut flakes

4 tbsp (40 g) fried shallot

To make the dressing, combine the chile powder, sugar, lime juice, tamari, salt and chili paste in a small bowl and stir until the sugar has dissolved.

To make the salad, heat the oil in a pan over medium heat, add the tempeh and fry for 3 minutes on each side until all sides are lightly browned, then remove from the pan and drain well.

Add the green mango, carrot, peanuts, red onion, green onion and dressing to a mixing bowl. Toss until well combined.

Make a bed of salad greens on a plate, top with the tempeh and spoon the salad mixture on top. Garnish with the coconut flakes and fried shallot.

Serve immediately for the freshest and best taste.

TIP: Green mango can be replaced with green apple.

WINGED BEAN SALAD

(YUM TUA PLU)

Winged beans are a rich source of protein, vitamins, minerals and an especially good source of vitamin A. It is one vegetable that offers a complete dose of nutrients to the body. This salad is a traditional dish from the central region of Thailand. The beans are blanched and tossed with coconut cream, roasted coconut flakes, crushed peanuts and a savory dressing. Finding winged beans outside of Thailand may be a challenge; I find that green beans or snap peas are a great substitute.

SERVES 4

DRESSING

2 tbsp (16 g) fried garlic

½ cup (110 g) brown sugar

4 tbsp (60 ml) lime juice

4 tbsp (60 ml) tamari

1 tbsp (15 g) Thai Home brand vegan Thai sweet chili paste (nam prik pao)

SALAD

3 cups (330 g) thinly sliced winged beans

¼ cup (60 ml) coconut cream

8 tbsp (37 g) roasted coconut flakes

8 tbsp (72 g) crushed roasted peanuts

2 cups (110 g) spring salad mix

8 tbsp (80 g) fried shallot, for garnish

To make the dressing, combine the fried garlic, sugar, lime juice, tamari and chili paste in a small bowl and stir until the sugar has dissolved.

To make the salad, prepare an ice bath. Bring a small pot of water to a boil over medium-high heat, add the beans and cook for 30 seconds. Transfer to the ice bath to stop the cooking, then drain well.

Place the coconut cream in a pan over medium heat and bring it to a boil, then remove from the heat and let cool.

Place the winged beans, coconut flakes and peanuts in a mixing bowl, add the coconut cream and the dressing and toss until well combined. Make a bed of greens on a plate and top with the salad mixture. Garnish with the fried shallot.

SPICY SOY CURLS TOM YUM SALAD

How about the famous Tom Yum soup transformed into a salad? The secret ingredient is vegan Thai sweet chili paste, or nam prik pao, *which is available at most Asian grocery stores and online. Be sure to buy one that does not contain shrimp paste, which is used in the original recipe for its umami flavor.*

SERVES 4

DRESSING

6 Thai chiles, finely chopped

1½ tbsp (12 g) minced garlic

¼ cup (55 g) brown sugar

2 tbsp (30 ml) lime juice

3 tbsp (45 ml) tamari

½ tsp salt

1 tbsp (15 g) Thai Home brand vegan Thai sweet chili paste (nam prik pao)

SALAD

3 cups (120 g) soy curls

1 tbsp (15 ml) vegetable oil

6 tbsp (29 g) finely sliced lemongrass

6 tbsp (16 g) finely sliced kaffir lime leaves

6 tbsp (60 g) finely sliced shallot

1 cup (16 g) chopped cilantro

1 cup (26 g) chopped mint leaves

8 grape tomatoes, halved

3 cups (165 g) spring salad mix

To make the dressing, combine the chiles, garlic, sugar, lime juice, tamari, salt and chili paste in a small bowl and stir until the sugar has dissolved.

To make the salad, soak the soy curls in water to soften per the package directions, drain well and let dry.

Heat the oil in a pan over medium heat, add the soy curls and fry for 1 to 2 minutes, then remove from the pan and drain well.

Place the soy curls, lemongrass, lime leaves, shallot, cilantro, mint, tomatoes and dressing in a mixing bowl, and toss to combine well. Make a bed of greens on a plate and top with the salad mixture.

GLASS NOODLE SOUP

(GANG JEUD WOONSEN)

Normally the word gang *in Thai means "curry" in English, but Gang Jeud Woonsen is the one exception. Gang Jeud Woosen, or Glass Noodle Soup, is simply a clear soup that cooks with veggies and mung bean noodles. Due to its light, mild flavor, this soup is typically served alongside spicy dishes, acting as a palate cleanser. It can also be eaten with tofu as a source of protein. Either way, you will enjoy it!*

SERVES 4

10 oz (283 g) Thai mung bean noodles

2 tbsp (30 ml) vegetable oil

2 tbsp (18 g) chopped garlic

15 cups (3.6 L) water

1½ cups (192 g) sliced carrot

1 tbsp (18 g) salt

1 tsp brown sugar

½ cup (120 ml) tamari

8 oz (228 g) soft tofu

8 oz (228 g) Napa cabbage, roughly chopped

3 stalks Chinese celery, cut into ¾" (2-cm) lengths, leaves chopped

½ cup (8 g) chopped cilantro, for garnish

½ tsp ground black pepper

Soak the noodles in cold water for about 10 minutes, drain and cut into 6-inch (15-cm) lengths.

Heat the oil in a soup pot over medium heat, then add the garlic and fry for 30 seconds. Add the water and bring to a boil over high heat. Once the water has come to a boil, add the carrot, salt, sugar and tamari and stir to mix well. Cook for 2 to 3 minutes, then add the soft tofu and Napa cabbage and cook for 3 more minutes or until the cabbage is soft. Add the celery and glass noodles and cook for about 30 seconds. Garnish with the cilantro and sprinkle with black pepper.

BANANA BLOSSOM TOM KHA SOUP

(TOM KHA HUE PLEE)

This soup has a sweet delicious flavor from the coconut milk and a unique, fragrant aroma from the lemongrass, galangal, lime leaves and cilantro. My favorite Tom Kha recipe is Tom Kha Hue Plee, which my mom always made. I remember this special banana blossom and coconut soup being served often. This simple, nourishing, tasty herbal soup is one I love to offer to friends and special guests.

SERVES 4

2 cups (480 ml) water

3 cups (720 ml) coconut milk

2" (5-cm) piece galangal, sliced into thin rounds

4 stalks lemongrass, sliced into 1" (2.5-cm) lengths

10 grape tomatoes

8 kaffir lime leaves

1 small young banana blossom, peeled and sliced ¼" (6 mm) thick

10 button mushrooms, halved

6 tbsp (90 ml) thin soy sauce

2 tbsp (25 g) sugar

6 tbsp (90 ml) fresh lime juice, plus more as needed

5 fresh Thai chiles, chopped, plus 2 chiles, hand-pounded, for garnish

½ cup (8 g) chopped cilantro

½ lime, cut into wedges

Place the water and coconut milk in a large pan and bring to a boil over high heat. Add the galangal, lemongrass, grape tomatoes, lime leaves and banana blossom. Boil for about 10 minutes or until the herbs release their flavor and the water turns light green. Add the mushrooms and boil for 3 more minutes.

Remove from the heat and add the soy sauce, sugar, lime juice and chiles. The flavor should be spicy and sour. If you like it more sour, add lime juice as needed. Garnish with the cilantro, lime wedges and pounded chiles. Remember that you don't eat the lemongrass, galangal or lime leaves, but they remain in in the soup for herbal flavor.

TIP: This soup tastes best hot because when it is cold, the coconut milk will separate and float up to the top.

LOTUS ROOT TOM YUM SOUP

(TOM YUM RAAK BUE)

Lotus root, or the rhizome of the lotus flower, is a root vegetable used in many Asian cuisines. It provides a crisp bite with sweet and savory flavors and has many health benefits as well. If you like spicy food, I recommend adding either a few Thai chile peppers (pounded) or a few drops of chile garlic oil at the end.

SERVES 4

4 cups (960 ml) water

2" (5-cm) piece galangal, sliced into thin rounds

4 stalks lemongrass, cut into 1" (2.5-cm) lengths

10 grape tomatoes

8 kaffir lime leaves

1 small lotus root (about 1 lb [454 g]), peeled and cut into ¼" (6-mm)-thick rounds

8 button mushrooms, halved

6 tbsp (90 ml) thin soy sauce or tamari

6 tbsp (90 ml) lime juice, plus more as needed

1 tbsp (15 g) Thai Home brand vegan Thai sweet chili paste (nam prik pao)

5 fresh Thai chiles, chopped, plus 2 chiles, hand-pounded, for garnish

½ cup (8 g) chopped cilantro

½ lime, cut into wedges

Place the water in a large pan and bring to a boil over high heat. Add the galangal, lemongrass, grape tomatoes, lime leaves and lotus root. Boil for about 10 minutes or until the herbs release their flavor and the water turns light green. Add the mushrooms and boil for 3 more minutes. Remove from the heat and add the soy sauce, lime juice, chili paste and chiles. The flavor should be spicy and sour. If you like it more sour, add more lime juice as needed. Garnish with the cilantro, pounded chiles and lime wedges.

Remember that you don't eat the lemongrass, galangal or lime leaves, but they remain in the soup for herbal flavor.

THE PEAR NOODLE SALAD

If noodles are one of your favorite dishes, then you should not miss this one! The Pear Noodle Salad is a popular noodle item at The Pear Juice Bar and Café, my restaurant in Portland, Oregon. With its fresh ingredients and wonderful peanut sauce, it's a healthier salad option that you will turn to again and again. This dish is inspired by Vietnamese noodle salad, or Ban Chay, but includes popular Thai herbs and vegetables and, of course, Thai peanut sauce.

SERVES 4 TO 6

SALAD

12 oz (336 g) pad Thai rice noodles

5 tbsp (75 ml) vegetable oil

6 oz (171 g) firm tofu, cut into 1" (2.5-cm) squares

2 tbsp (16 g) minced garlic

½ cup (36 g) shredded cabbage

½ cup (55 g) shredded carrot

1 cup (50 g) fresh bean sprouts

2 cups (220 g) spring salad mix

3 handfuls of Thai basil

6 tbsp (54 g) crushed peanuts

PEANUT DRESSING

½ cup (130 g) natural peanut butter

1 cup (220 g) brown sugar

½ cup (120 ml) water

½ cup (120 ml) apple cider vinegar

1 tbsp (15 ml) tamari

1 tbsp (18 g) salt

2 tbsp (30 ml) chili garlic sauce

To make the salad, soak the noodles in enough cold water to cover for 1 hour if using fresh noodles or 3 hours if using dried, then drain.

To make the peanut dressing, combine the peanut butter, brown sugar, water, apple cider vinegar, tamari, salt and chili garlic sauce in a saucepan over medium heat and cook, stirring, until the sugar has dissolved, then simmer for 2 to 3 minutes or until the sauce is thick.

Heat the oil in a pan over medium heat, add the tofu and fry for about 6 minutes or until all the sides are lightly brown, then remove from the pan and drain well. Use the same oil to fry the garlic until golden brown, 10 seconds, then remove from the pan and drain well.

Bring a pot of water to a boil over medium-high heat, add the rice noodles and cook for 45 seconds, then quickly remove from the pot and drain well.

Add the cooked noodles to a mixing bowl, then add the crispy garlic and 4 tablespoons (60 ml) of the peanut dressing and toss until well combined. Transfer to a bowl and top with the fried tofu, cabbage, carrot, bean sprouts, salad mix, Thai basil and crushed peanuts.

TIP: Add more peanut dressing if you like more sauce or add chopped fresh chiles if you like more spice.

EIGHT INCREDIBLE EVERYDAY CURRY RECIPES

Curry, or *gang* in Thai, is the mixing of concentrated Thai curry paste in either water or coconut milk. Thai curry paste can be classified by the type and amount of spices used in that curry paste. For example, Massaman curry has the most spices when compared with other curry pastes. Green curry paste has fresh green chile peppers, but red curry paste has dried red chile peppers as the key ingredient.

The traditional way of cooking a Thai curry is to pound the curry paste with fresh herbs and other ingredients just before cooking, and then pour the coconut milk right from the recently picked coconut. Today, making curry is fast, simple and still delicious with a jar of Thai curry paste and a box of coconut milk from the supermarket. Be sure to read the curry paste ingredients list because most curry pastes contain shrimp paste and may not be available as a vegan product. Also keep in mind that most curry pastes already contain salt, so always taste your curry before adding salt and soy sauce.

AVOCADO GREEN CURRY

Green curry is the most popular curry in Thai food, both for Thai people and for foreigners. The main ingredient of this dish is herbal green curry paste, a recipe transferred in my family from generation to generation.

SERVES 4

8 oz (228 g) kabocha squash, peeled and cut into ½" (1.3-cm) squares

1 tbsp (15 ml) coconut oil

½ cup (120 g) Thai Home brand vegan Thai green curry paste, or to taste

2½ cups (600 ml) coconut milk

1 red bell pepper, cut into ½" (1.3-cm) squares

1 green bell pepper, cut into ½" (1.3-cm) squares

8 oz (228 g) firm tofu, cut into 1" (2.5-cm) squares

1 cup (240 ml) vegetable broth

¾ cup (165 g) brown sugar

¼ cup (60 ml) tamari

2 handfuls of Thai basil

2 medium ripe avocados, peeled, pitted and cut into 8 even pieces

1 cup (63 g) snow peas

Steamed jasmine rice, brown rice or vermicelli, for serving

Bring a small pot of water to a boil over medium-high heat, add the kabocha squash and cook for 8 minutes. Drain the water and let cool.

Heat the oil in a large saucepan over medium heat, add the green curry paste and cook, stirring, for about 1 minute, then add the coconut milk and stir until well combined. Heat the mixture for a few more minutes or until the oil begins to separate. Add the kabocha squash, red and green bell peppers, tofu and vegetable broth, increase the heat to high and bring to a boil. Once it's boiling, continue cooking for 5 more minutes, then add the sugar, tamari, Thai basil, avocados and snow peas, reduce to a simmer and cook for 6 more minutes.

Serve with steamed jasmine white or brown rice or vermicelli.

TIP: If you want more green color for your curry but don't want to add more spice, process cilantro and water in a blender until smooth and then use the mixture to make the dish greener.

MANGO RED CURRY

If original red curry sounds a bit boring to you, why not try adding a twist with mango? I've been cooking mango in red curry for a long time, and the blend of sweet and sour mango with the salty and savory red curry sauce makes a perfect combination. In this recipe, feel free to change up the vegetables that you'd like, as long as you cut them all about the same size. Serve with steamed jasmine rice for a warm, comforting and perfect food for cool days.

SERVES 4

8 oz (228 g) kabocha squash, peeled and cut into ½" (1.3-cm) squares

1 tbsp (15 ml) coconut oil

½ cup (120 g) Thai Home brand vegan Thai red curry paste, or to taste

2½ cups (600 ml) coconut milk

1 red bell pepper, cut into ½" (1.3-cm) squares

1 green bell pepper, cut into ½" (1.3-cm) squares

8 oz (228 g) firm tofu, cut into 1" (2.5-cm) squares

1 cup (240 ml) vegetable broth

16 oz (456 g) medium-size ripe mango, peeled and cut into ½" (1.3-cm) squares

½ cup (110 g) brown sugar

¼ cup (60 ml) tamari

2 handfuls of Thai basil

1 cup (63 g) snow peas

Steamed jasmine rice, for serving

Bring a small pot of water to a boil over medium-high heat, add the kabocha squash and cook for 8 minutes. Drain the water and let cool.

Heat the oil in a large saucepan over medium heat, add the red curry paste and cook, stirring, for about 1 minute, then add the coconut milk and stir until well combined. Heat the mixture for a few more minutes or until the oil begins to separate. Add the kabocha squash, red and green bell peppers, tofu and vegetable broth, increase the heat to high and bring to a boil. Once it's boiling, continue cooking for 5 more minutes, then add the mango, sugar, tamari, Thai basil and snow peas, reduce to a simmer and cook for 6 more minutes.

Serve with steamed jasmine rice.

TARO-POTATO MASSAMAN CURRY

When it comes to the world's most delicious Thai food, it must be Massaman curry. Massaman curry is influenced by Persians who immigrated to Thailand. Thai people incorporated Massaman curry into their cuisine and tinkered with it until it tasted just right for the Thai palate: sweet, salty and a little bit sour with the aromatic scent of cinnamon and spices. To make perfect Massaman curry, do not forgo the key ingredients: potato, tomato, peanut, tamarind juice and, of course, Massaman curry paste.

SERVES 4

8 oz (228 g) potato, cut into 1" (2.5-cm) squares

8 oz (228 g) taro, cut into 1" (2.5-cm) squares

1 tbsp (15 ml) coconut oil

½ cup (120 g) Thai Home brand vegan Thai Massaman curry paste, or to taste

2½ cups (600 ml) coconut milk

½ cup (64 g) sliced carrot

4 oz (114 g) yellow onion, cut into 1" (2.5-cm) squares

8 oz (228 g) firm tofu, cut into 1" (2.5-cm) squares

10 cherry tomatoes

1 cup (240 ml) vegetable broth

¾ cup (165 g) brown sugar

¼ cup (60 ml) tamari

2 tbsp (18 g) roasted peanuts

2 tbsp (30 ml) tamarind juice

Roti, for serving

Pickled cucumber, for serving

Bring a small pot of water to a boil over medium-high heat, add the potato and taro and cook for 8 minutes. Drain the water and let cool.

Heat the oil in a large saucepan over medium heat, add the Massaman curry paste and cook, stirring, for about 1 minute, then add the coconut milk and stir until well combined. Heat the mixture for a few more minutes or until the oil begins to separate. Add the cooked potato, taro, carrot, yellow onion, tofu, cherry tomatoes and vegetable broth, increase the heat to high and bring to a boil. Once it's boiling, continue cooking for 5 more minutes, then add the sugar, tamari, peanuts and tamarind juice, reduce to a simmer and cook for 6 more minutes.

Serve with roti (Indian flatbread) and pickled cucumber.

PINEAPPLE-TEMPEH CURRY

Pineapple curry is one of the original Thai curry dishes that is commonly available everywhere in Thailand. This curry taste has a unique sweet and sour flavor from the pineapple and a fragrant and spicy flavor from the red curry paste and coconut milk.

SERVES 4

1 cup (240 ml) vegetable oil

12 oz (342 g) tempeh, cut into ½" (1.3-cm) squares

1 tbsp (15 ml) coconut oil

½ cup (120 g) Thai Home brand vegan Thai red curry paste, or to taste

2½ cups (600 ml) coconut milk

18 oz (500 g) pineapple, cut into ½" (1.3-cm) squares

15 cherry tomatoes

1 cup (240 ml) vegetable broth

½ cup (110 g) brown sugar

¼ cup (60 ml) tamari

2 handfuls of Thai basil

Steamed jasmine or brown rice, for serving

Heat the vegetable oil in a pan over medium heat, add the tempeh and fry for about 3 minutes on each side until all the sides are lightly brown. Remove from the pan and drain well.

Heat the coconut oil in a large saucepan over medium heat, add the red curry paste and cook, stirring, for about 1 minute, then add the coconut milk and stir until well combined. Heat the mixture for a few more minutes or until the oil begins to separate. Add the pineapple, cherry tomatoes and vegetable broth, increase the heat to high and bring to a boil. Once it's boiling, continue cooking for 5 more minutes, then add the sugar, tamari, Thai basil and tempeh, reduce to a simmer and cook for 6 more minutes.

Serve with steamed white jasmine or brown rice.

ASSORTED MUSHROOMS CURRY

For those who love mushrooms, this assorted mushroom curry is full of flavor and health benefits. Mushrooms are high in fiber and low in calories, so this dish will fill you up while keeping calories low. Don't care for mushrooms? Cauliflower, sweet potato, zucchini and broccoli are all delicious substitutes.

SERVES 4

6 oz (171 g) white mushrooms

6 oz (171 g) beech mushrooms

6 oz (171 g) shiitake mushrooms

6 oz (171 g) oyster mushrooms

1 tbsp (15 ml) coconut oil

½ cup (120 g) Thai Home brand vegan Thai red curry paste, or to taste

2½ cups (600 ml) coconut milk

1 red bell pepper, cut into ½" (1.3-cm) squares

1 green bell pepper, cut into ½" (1.3-cm) squares

1 cup (240 ml) vegetable broth

½ cup (110 g) brown sugar

¼ cup (60 ml) tamari

2 handfuls of Thai basil

Steamed jasmine or brown rice, for serving

Clean and cut the mushrooms into bite-size pieces. Heat the oil in a large saucepan over medium heat, add the red curry paste and cook, stirring, for about 1 minute, then add the coconut milk and stir well until combined. Heat the mixture for a few more minutes or until the oil begins to separate. Add the mushrooms, red and green bell peppers and vegetable broth, increase the heat to high and bring to a boil. Once it's boiling, add the sugar, tamari and Thai basil, reduce to a simmer and cook for 6 more minutes.

Serve with steamed white jasmine or brown rice.

PANANG TOFU

Panang curry is pretty similar to red curry, but Panang curry is thick, creamy and usually less spicy than traditional red curry. It also has a unique, fragrant flavor from the addition of kaffir lime leaves. Panang in Thai cooking normally uses fresh Thai red chile peppers instead of red and green bell peppers. If you dare to try the heat of Thai chile peppers, go for it!

SERVES 4

1 tbsp (15 ml) coconut oil

¼ cup (60 g) Thai Home brand vegan Thai Panang curry paste, or to taste

1½ cups (360 ml) coconut milk

12 oz (342 g) firm tofu, cut into ½" (1.3-cm) squares

1 red bell pepper, cut into ½" (1.3-cm) squares

1 green bell pepper, cut into ½" (1.3-cm) squares

4 young peppercorn stalks

¼ cup (55 g) brown sugar

3 tbsp (45 ml) tamari

2 handfuls of Thai basil

2 tbsp (5 g) shredded kaffir lime leaves

Steamed jasmine or brown rice, for serving

Heat the coconut oil in a large saucepan over medium heat, add the Panang curry paste and cook, stirring, for about 1 minute, then add the coconut milk and stir until well combined. Heat the mixture for a few more minutes or until the oil begins to separate. Add the tofu, red and green bell peppers and peppercorn stalks, increase the heat to high and bring to a boil. Once it's boiling, continue cooking for 5 more minutes, then add the sugar, tamari and Thai basil, reduce to a simmer and cook for 6 more minutes. Sprinkle with the lime leaves.

Serve with steamed white jasmine or brown rice.

KABOCHA SQUASH CURRY

Kabocha, a type of winter squash, is a popular squash used in many Asian cuisines for both sweet and savory dishes. The sweet taste of kabocha squash simmering in red curry coconut milk makes it a perfect dish for a chilly autumn or winter day. If you can't find kabocha squash at your local supermarket, butternut squash is a good substitute.

SERVES 4

16 oz (456 g) kabocha squash, peeled and cut into ½" (1.3-cm) squares

1 tbsp (15 ml) coconut oil

½ cup (120 g) Thai Home brand vegan Thai red curry paste, or to taste

2½ cups (600 ml) coconut milk

8 kaffir lime leaves

¾ cup (180 ml) vegetable broth

½ cup (110 g) brown sugar

¼ cup (60 ml) tamari

2 handfuls of Thai basil

Steamed jasmine or brown rice, for serving

Bring a small pot of water to a boil over medium-high heat, add the kabocha squash and cook for 8 minutes. Drain the water and let cool.

Heat the coconut oil in a large saucepan over medium heat, add the red curry paste and cook, stirring, for about 1 minute, then add the coconut milk and stir until well combined. Heat the mixture for a few more minutes or until the oil begins to separate. Add the kabocha squash, lime leaves and vegetable broth, increase the heat to high and bring to a boil. Once it's boiling, continue cooking for 5 more minutes, then add the sugar, tamari and Thai basil, reduce to a simmer and cook for 6 more minutes.

Serve with steamed white jasmine or brown rice.

JUNGLE CURRY

(GANG PAH)

Traditional Thai jungle curry is one of the few curry dishes without coconut milk. Jungle curry features a salty but not sweet flavor profile. This dish originated in the central part of Thailand, and because my mom was born in that region, in Ang Thong province, it is one of her favorite dishes.

SERVES 4

10 oz (285 g) kabocha squash, peeled and cut into ½" (1.3-cm) squares

10 Thai eggplants, halved (optional)

1 tbsp (15 ml) coconut oil

½ cup (120 g) Thai Home brand vegan Thai red curry paste, or to taste

3 cups (720 ml) vegetable broth

1 red bell pepper, cut into ½" (1.3-cm) squares

1 green bell pepper, cut into ½" (1.3-cm) squares

½ cup (76 g) bamboo shoot, sliced

5 kaffir lime leaves

4 young peppercorn stalks

10 pieces whole baby corn

7 button mushrooms, halved

½ cup (110 g) brown sugar

¼ cup (60 ml) tamari

2 handfuls of Thai basil

1 cup (63 g) snow peas

Steamed jasmine or brown rice, for serving

Bring a small pot of water to a boil over medium-high heat, add the kabocha squash and eggplants, if using, and cook for 8 minutes. Drain the water and let cool.

Heat the coconut oil in a large saucepan over medium heat, add the red curry paste and cook, stirring, for about 1 minute, then add the vegetable broth and stir until well combined. Add the kabocha squash, eggplants (if using), red and green bell peppers, bamboo shoot, lime leaves, peppercorn stalks, baby corn and mushrooms, increase the heat to high and bring to a boil. Once it's boiling, continue cooking for 5 more minutes, then add the sugar, tamari, Thai basil and snow peas, reduce to a simmer and cook for 6 more minutes.

Serve with steamed white jasmine or brown rice.

DELICIOUS THAI DESSERTS

In Thailand, we use bananas and all parts of the banana tree in various types of food, including desserts. Not only are bananas sweet and delicious, but they are also rich in beneficial vitamins and minerals. Plus, bananas are available throughout the year, so there is no need to wait to try any of these desserts! Due to their availability in Thailand, cultivated bananas, or *kluai namwa*, are most often used. This banana is sweet and smooth in texture, and thus can be processed in many ways. Although finding *kluai namwa* outside of Thailand might be challenging, regular bananas can be substituted. Keep in mind, though, that due to different textures of banana varieties, one might cook faster than another, so adjust the cooking time as necessary.

Coconut products are also another popular ingredient for Thai desserts, simply because coconuts are widely grown in Southeast Asia and are delicious. Coconut milk has a fragrant sweetness that is more nuanced than cane sugar and thus brings new flavors to Thai desserts.

In this chapter, we will use a lot of coconut milk as a key ingredient. Be sure to pick a type that is used for food or dessert, as regular coconut milk beverage is too light and cannot be substituted.

MANGO STICKY RICE

(KHAO NEAW MA MAUNG)

Mango sticky rice is a must-eat when you visit Thailand. With the sweet mango served on top of fragrant coconut sticky rice, this dish is so refreshing and comforting. There are many different types of mango, but Champagne mango is my favorite. Not only is it super sweet and colorful, but it is also less fibrous compared to other mango varieties. My way of eating mango sticky rice is to add a scoop of coconut ice cream and sprinkle it with crispy roasted coconut chips. You'll need a traditional Thai sticky rice steamer basket, available at most Asian grocery stores or online.

SERVES 4 OR 5

STICKY RICE

4 cups (768 g) sticky rice

3 cups (720 ml) coconut milk

1 tsp salt

1 cup (200 g) palm sugar

COCONUT TOPPING

1½ cups (360 ml) coconut milk

1 tsp rice flour

½ tsp salt

4 or 5 sweet Champagne mangoes, peeled, pitted and sliced

Toasted sesame seed, for garnish (optional)

Fresh mint leaves, for garnish (optional)

To make the sticky rice, place the rice in a large bowl, cover with cold water and let soak for 3 hours. Drain the water and place the rice in a traditional Thai sticky rice steamer basket over boiling water in a large pot. There should be at least several inches (15 cm) of empty space between the basket and the boiling water. Make sure you place the lid to cover the basket for better steaming. Cook the rice for 20 minutes, then flip over the rice and cook through for 10 more minutes.

Meanwhile, add the coconut milk to a small pot over medium heat and add the salt and palm sugar and stir until the sugar has dissolved and the mixture is well combined.

Once the sticky rice is tender but not overcooked, pour it into a large bowl. Add the coconut milk mixture to the rice and mix well. Wrap the bowl with plastic wrap and leave the mixture for 30 minutes to allow the rice to absorb the coconut milk mixture.

To make the coconut topping, add the coconut milk to a pan and bring to a boil over high heat. Add the rice flour and salt, then stir well until dissolved and combined.

To garnish and serve, place the sticky rice on a plate, add sliced sweet mango on top of the rice, then top the mango with the sauce, sprinkle with toasted sesame seeds and garnish with fresh mint leaves, if desired.

TIP: You can keep leftover coconut sticky rice in a covered container in the refrigerator or freezer and rewarm in the microwave for 1 to 2 minutes before serving.

BANANA SPRING ROLLS

The best banana spring rolls are crispy and crunchy on the outside and sweet on the inside. Some people like to serve them cut in half to make them easier to eat. I prefer my banana rolls not too sweet, but you can always sprinkle yours with maple syrup, jam, powdered sugar or toasted coconut flakes. You can also freeze them uncooked and then fry them up quickly at your next party.

MAKES 4 ROLLS

2 tbsp (16 g) tapioca flour

1 tbsp (15 ml) water

1 medium ripe banana

4 fresh spring roll wrappers, 8" (20-cm) square

2 cups (480 ml) vegetable oil

2 tsp (5 g) icing sugar

1 tbsp (5 g) toasted coconut flakes

Make a sticky paste by mixing the tapioca flour and water in a small bowl. Peel the banana and cut in half lengthwise, then cut in half again to make 4 quarters. Lay the spring roll wrappers on a cutting board and place one banana quarter in a line along its center. Roll the banana tightly to the end, dip your finger in the sticky paste and use it to seal the edge.

Pour the oil into a deep pot over medium heat and bring the oil to 350°F (180°C). Fry the banana rolls until the skin is golden brown and crunchy, about 5 minutes. Sprinkle with icing sugar and toasted coconut flakes.

CORN AND TAPIOCA PUDDING

This dessert is a sweet corn and tapioca pudding simmered in a sweet and delicious coconut milk sauce. It is very easy to prepare and tastes great as well!

SERVES 4

¼ cup (38 g) small white tapioca pearls

3 cups (720 ml) water

3½ cups (840 ml) coconut milk

2 cups (289 g) cooked fresh or frozen sweet corn

½ cup (100 g) sugar

¼ tsp salt

Place the tapioca pearls in a small bowl, cover with cold water by 1 inch (2.5 cm) and soak for 1 minute, then drain. Add the 3 cups (720 ml) of water to a pan, place over medium-high heat and bring to a boil. Add the drained tapioca and cook for 7 minutes, stirring to prevent scorching on the bottom. Drain and let cool.

Add the coconut milk, corn, sugar and salt to another pot and stir to combine. Bring to a boil over medium-high heat, then reduce the heat to a simmer, add the cooked tapioca, stir well and cook for 2 minutes. Taste and adjust the salt or sugar if needed. Serve hot or cold.

TIP: You can refrigerate the pudding for up to 48 hours, and then warm it in the microwave for about 1 minute before serving; add more water if it's too thick.

SWEET BANANAS

The Thai banana called gluay nam wah *is a key ingredient in this recipe and can be found in Asian grocery stores. This dessert is very simple. The banana is cooked in a sweet syrup and served with slightly salty coconut milk on top to balance the sweetness. Not only can you can eat this sweet banana as a dessert, but during a hot summer day it can be a cool topping to add to ice cream as well.*

SERVES 5

FOR THE COCONUT TOPPING

2½ cups (600 ml) coconut milk

1½ tsp (9 g) salt

1 tsp rice flour

¼ cup (60 ml) water

10 medium-size ripe Thai bananas

8 cups (1.9 L) water

7 cups (1.5 kg) brown sugar

¼ tsp salt

To make the coconut topping, combine the coconut milk and salt in a pot and bring to a boil over medium heat. Mix the rice flour with the water, then add to the boiling coconut milk. Stir to combine and cook for 3 minutes.

Peel the bananas. Cut each in half lengthwise and then cut in half again to get 4 quarters from each banana.

Add the water, brown sugar and salt to a stainless-steel pot over low heat. Stir until the sugar dissolves and forms a syrup. Add the cut bananas to the syrup and cook over very low heat for about 2 hours, or until the bananas turn reddish in color. Remove from the syrup and drain. Let cool.

Serve with the coconut topping at room temperature.

BANANAS IN COCONUT MILK

In Thailand, meals are usually finished with fresh fruit, so serving a sweet dish like bananas in coconut milk at the end of a meal is common. You can also enjoy eating this as a snack. This recipe is one of the simplest Thai desserts you can make—bananas simply simmered in sweet coconut milk to create a flavorful dessert.

SERVES 2 OR 3

5 medium-size ripe Thai bananas
3 cups (720 ml) coconut milk
1 cup (240 ml) water
½ cup (100 g) sugar
½ tsp salt

Peel the bananas. Cut each in half lengthwise and then cut in half again to get 4 quarters from each banana.

Add the coconut milk and water to a stainless-steel pot. Bring to a boil over medium heat. Add the sugar and salt and stir until dissolved. Add the cut bananas to the mixture and cook over medium heat for 10 to 15 minutes. Serve hot or at room temperature.

BLACK STICKY RICE PUDDING

This dish calls for glutinous black rice, also known as black sticky rice, or khao neaw dum. *Black sticky rice is slightly sweet by nature and coconut milk adds a wonderful flavor to it. This pudding not only gives you a satisfying dessert but it is also high in fiber and nutrients. To make this dish, be sure to plan ahead, because you have to soak the sticky rice in water overnight.*

SERVES 4

¼ cup (50 g) black sticky rice, soaked overnight in enough water to cover

¾ cup (150 g) white sticky rice, soaked overnight in enough water to cover

3 cups plus 2 tbsp (750 ml) water, divided

½ cup (100 g) sugar, or to taste

1 cup (200 g) fresh Thai young coconut meat (canned or frozen is fine if you can't find fresh)

1 tsp corn flour

COCONUT TOPPING

1½ cups (360 ml) coconut milk

1 tsp rice flour

½ tsp salt

Toasted sesame seeds, for garnish (optional)

When ready to cook, drain the sticky rice from the soaking water. Place the sticky rices in a pot, add 3 cups (720 ml) of the water and cook over medium heat until the rice is cooked and the water has been absorbed, 30 minutes. Stir to make sure there is no burning rice on the bottom, and add more water if needed. Once the rice is cooked, add the sugar and coconut meat and mix well.

Mix the corn flour with the remaining 2 tablespoons (30 ml) of water in a small bowl, then add to the sticky rice and stir to combine. Remove from the heat and let cool.

To make the coconut topping, add the coconut milk to a pan and bring to a boil over medium-high heat. Add the rice flour and salt, and stir until well combined and dissolved.

Serve the sweet sticky rice in bowls and top with the coconut sauce. Sprinkle with toasted sesame seeds, if desired.

THAI TEAS AND TROPICAL SMOOTHIES

Thai iced tea is an orange-hued cold beverage prepared with black tea, sugar and milk. Its origin is unknown, but Thai tea recipes are very similar to Indian chai. Thai tea can be served hot or cold, but Thai iced tea is the most popular due to the hot climate of the region. In Thailand, you can find Thai iced tea easily at street vendors and market stalls, where the tea is typically poured over crushed ice in a clear plastic bag or tall plastic cup.

My favorite tropical fruit, dragon fruit (or pitaya), is a fruit in the cactus family that is widely grown in Southeast Asia. Its texture is like kiwi and it is mildly sweet. There are many different colors, but the pink one is commonly used in smoothies and other drinks. Not only does dragon fruit add beautiful color to your smoothies, but it's also high in nutrients and loaded with fiber.

To make the tea recipes, you'll need a Thai tea filter cloth bag (available at most Thai or Asian grocery stores or online) and two stainless-steel coffee containers (glass is okay to use but stainless steel will contain the heat for much longer). Boxed coconut milk is the best milk for vegan Thai tea, as it is very rich and creamy.

VEGAN THAI TEA

Famous Thai tea is now available in a vegan version. Thai iced tea is a delicious and refreshing Thai drink made from Thai tea mix, sugar and condensed milk. It's not only popular in Thailand but in Southeast Asia and the United States as well. Preparing Thai iced tea is very easy and requires just a few ingredients. In this recipe, coconut milk is the substitution to the condensed and evaporated milk in the original Thai tea.

SERVES 5 OR 6

1 cup (32 g) Thai tea mix (Thai black tea)

3 cups (720 ml) boiling water

PER TEA SHOT

2 tbsp (25 g) sugar

1 oz (30 ml) vegan condensed coconut milk

Ice cubes

2 oz (60 ml) coconut barista milk

Add the Thai tea mix to a filter bag, then add the boiling water. Pour the tea through the filter bag between two stainless-steel containers 5 or 6 times, then let the tea sit for about 10 minutes and strain. You can leave it longer if you like stronger tea.

To make one tea shot, in a teacup, mix 3 ounces (90 ml) of the hot filtered Thai tea with the sugar and stir well until the sugar has dissolved. Add the vegan condensed milk and stir until combined. Fill a 16-ounce (480-ml) glass with ice cubes, then pour in the tea mixture. Top with the coconut barista milk. Add more coconut milk if you like it lighter.

TIPS: It is best to drink Thai tea fresh, but you can keep it (without ice) in the refrigerator for up to 4 days.

You can use paper tea bags with a string if a traditional Thai filter tea bag is not available.

VEGAN THAI ICED COFFEE

The world-famous Thai iced coffee has three main ingredients: Thai coffee grounds, sugar and condensed milk. I use coconut milk instead of regular milk in this recipe. I found that coconut milk is best for Thai iced coffee, but you can use any plant milk of choice, such as almond milk, hemp milk or oat milk.

SERVES 6 OR 7

1 cup (32 g) Thai coffee mix (oliang powder)

4 cups (940 ml) boiling water

PER COFFEE SHOT

2 tbsp (25 g) sugar

1 oz (30 ml) vegan condensed coconut milk

Ice cubes

2 oz (60 ml) coconut barista milk (or your milk of choice)

Add the coffee powder to a filter bag, then add the boiling water. Let the coffee brew for about 10 minutes, then strain. You can leave it longer if you like stronger coffee.

To make one coffee shot, in a coffee cup, mix 3 ounces (90 ml) of the hot filtered coffee with the sugar and stir well until the sugar has dissolved. Add the vegan condensed milk and stir until all combined. Fill a 16-ounce (480-ml) glass with ice cubes, then pour in the coffee mixture. Top with the coconut barista milk. Add more coconut milk if you like it lighter.

TIP: You can use paper tea bags with a string if a traditional Thai filter tea bag is not available.

VEGAN THAI ICED GREEN TEA

Thai food is quite spicy, so eating it with a glass of Thai iced green tea would be a great idea. This sweet milk drink can help soothe the heat when you're overloaded with Thai spices. Be careful to drink it early in the day, as it does have quite a bit of caffeine that may keep you awake at night. I find coconut milk is best for Thai iced green tea, but you can use any plant milk of your choice.

SERVES 5 OR 6

1 cup (32 g) Thai green tea mix

3 cups (720 ml) boiling water

PER TEA SHOT

2 tbsp (25 g) sugar

1 oz (30 ml) vegan condensed coconut milk

Ice cubes

2 oz (60 ml) coconut barista milk

Add the green tea mix to a filter bag, then add the boiling water. Pour the tea through the filter bag between two stainless-steel containers 5 or 6 times, then let the tea sit for about 10 minutes and strain. You can leave it longer if you like stronger tea.

To make one shot of tea, in a teacup, mix 3 ounces (90 ml) of the hot filtered tea with the sugar and stir well until the sugar has dissolved. Add the vegan condensed milk and stir until combined. Fill a 16-ounce (480-ml) glass with ice cubes, then pour in the tea mixture. Top with the coconut barista milk. Add more coconut milk if you like it lighter.

TIP: You can use paper tea bags with a string if a traditional Thai filter tea bag is not available.

THAI LIME ICED TEA

Thai tea is a popular traditional beverage in Thailand and is served either hot or cold. It's generally prepared with sugar and milk. This recipe is perfect for vegans because it does not contain any milk. Green lime is a key ingredient for this iced tea. Simply prepare the tea as you ordinarily would, add sugar to the hot tea, squeeze in the lime juice and pour it over ice. This makes a perfect summer drink.

SERVES 5 OR 6

1 cup (32 g) Thai tea mix (Thai black tea)

3 cups (720 ml) boiling water

Add the Thai black tea to a filter bag, then add the boiling water. Pour the tea through the filter bag between two stainless-steel containers 5 or 6 times, then let the tea sit for about 10 minutes and strain. You can leave it longer if you like stronger tea.

PER TEA SHOT

2 tbsp (25 g) sugar

Juice of 1 lime

Ice cubes

1 mint leaf

To make one shot of tea, in a teacup, mix 3 ounces (90 ml) of the hot filtered tea with the sugar and stir well until the sugar has dissolved. Add the lime juice and mix well. Fill a 16-ounce (480-ml) glass with ice cubes, then pour the tea mixture over. Top with a mint leaf for a refreshing scent.

TIPS: It is best to drink Thai tea fresh, but you can keep it (without ice) in the refrigerator for up to 4 days.

You can use paper tea bags with a string if a traditional Thai filter tea bag is not available.

MANGO MADNESS

This mango smoothie is best in the summertime and is perfect for a healthy breakfast or midafternoon snack. It takes less than 5 minutes to prepare and tastes amazing.

SERVES 2

2 cups (330 g) frozen mango chunks

2 cups (300 g) frozen chopped banana

1 cup (245 g) frozen pineapple chunks

2 tbsp (12 g) coconut flakes

2 cups (480 ml) coconut water

Fresh mango chunks, for garnish (optional)

Mint leaves, for garnish (optional)

Place the frozen mango, banana, pineapple, coconut flakes and coconut water in a blender. Blend until completely smooth. If the mixture is too thick, add more coconut water. Pour into a 16-ounce (480-ml) Mason jar to serve, garnished with fresh mango chunks and a mint leaf, if desired.

TIP: If you like a milkier drink, you can substitute the coconut water with coconut milk.

PHUKET COCONUT SHAKE

Treat yourself to this rich and creamy vegan smoothie. It is named after Phuket, the most famous island in Thailand. As we know by now, in Thailand, coconut is in almost every meal and appears in dishes ranging from sweets to curries. Coconut juice is also a perfect beverage that is full of nutrients and electrolytes. It can be served alone or mixed with other fruits for a more filling drink.

SERVES 2

2 fresh Thai young coconuts

4 oz (120 ml) agave or date syrup

4 oz (120 ml) coconut cream

½ tsp salt

1 cup (200 g) ice

Coconut jelly, for garnish (optional)

Orchid flowers, for garnish (optional)

Open the coconut and transfer the coconut water and the coconut meat to a blender. Add the agave, coconut cream, salt and ice and blend until completely smooth. Pour the smoothie back into the empty coconut shell or a 16-ounce (480-ml) Mason jar to serve, garnished with coconut jelly and an orchid flower, if desired.

PASSION FRUIT AND MANGO SMOOTHIE

Turn mango and passion fruit into this heavenly tropical smoothie. This recipe is a nutritious way to start your day because it is full of vitamins, high in antioxidants and low in fat. This smoothie is also ideal for a hot summer day.

SERVES 2

2 cups (330 g) frozen mango chunks

14 oz (420 ml) passion fruit puree

2 cups (480 ml) coconut milk

2 tbsp (30 ml) agave nectar

1 cup (200 g) ice

Mint leaves, for garnish (optional)

Place the frozen mango, passion fruit puree, coconut milk, agave and ice in a blender. Blend until completely smooth. Pour into a 16-ounce (480-ml) Mason jar to serve, garnished with mint, if desired.

PITAYA BREAKFAST SMOOTHIE

Pitaya, also called dragon fruit or strawberry pear, is a tropical fruit known for its vibrant red skin and sweet, seed-speckled pulp. Its acclaimed superfood powers have made it popular among foodies and the health conscious. Pitaya is high in nutrients, essential vitamins and minerals, fiber and antioxidants. This recipe is definitely a good choice for a superfood smoothie to start your day.

SERVES 2

3 cups (480 g) frozen pitaya chunks

2 cups (300 g) frozen chopped banana

3 cups (720 ml) coconut water

4 tbsp (32 g) granola, for garnish (optional)

2 tbsp (16 g) blueberries, for garnish (optional)

Place the frozen pitaya chunks, banana and coconut water in a blender. Blend until completely smooth. Pour into a 16-ounce (480-ml) Mason jar to serve, garnished with granola and blueberries, if desired.

RESOURCES

TIPS FOR SHOPPING FOR THAI INGREDIENTS

Most Thai specialty ingredients listed in this book can be found in Asian grocery stores. Be aware that this may not be one-stop shopping, although you may be fortunate to have a fantastic store nearby that has everything you need. Plan on spending a little time to get the best ingredients for your meal.

If you plan to cook Asian food on a regular basis, take a day to visit as many Asian markets in your area as possible. You will learn what each store carries and where to get what you need for your next cooking day.

ASIAN GROCERY STORES

Asian grocery stores are divided into three zones, just like other supermarkets:

Fresh produce: Here you can find most of the herbs needed for these recipes, such as kaffir lime leaves, galangal, lemongrass, cilantro, spring onions, sweet basil, banana flowers and more. Fresh fruits and vegetables can also be found in this section, including limes, Japanese and Chinese eggplant, kabocha squash, mangoes, pineapple, papaya—both ripe and green—and various other exotic fruits and vegetables.

Dry goods: Here you can find certain types of specialty ingredients that are not available in regular supermarkets, such as curry pastes, certain beans, rice, noodles and so forth.

Frozen products: You can also find most herbs like galangal, lemongrass, kaffir lime and Thai chiles here. This is my favorite section during the winter, when the fresh produce I want isn't always available.

ONLINE RETAILERS

Most Asian specialty ingredients, as well as authentic cooking utensils and equipment, are available on Amazon. My vegan curry pastes from Thai Home products, on which my recipes are based, are also available there.

ACKNOWLEDGMENTS

I couldn't have made this cookbook without my team at Kati Portland, The Pear Café, Thai Home Curry Paste and the Jansala family.

Most importantly, I would like to give credit to our customers who have supported our business over the past few years. Without any of you guys we would not be able to continue the work that we love. Thanks again for your love and support.

Thank you to my pharmacy coworkers for always creating a fun, positive and inspiring workspace.

Special thanks to Lauren Knowles, my editor, and Karen Levy, my copyeditor, without whom this cookbook would not be possible. To Laura Gallant, the designer, and Meg Baskis, my cookbook's creative director, thanks for your creative ideas and design as well as your time putting this book together. To Toni Zernik, my photographer, thank you for creating such fantastic photography that can make anybody hungry at first sight.

And lastly, a huge thank you to my mom, Renoo Jansala, for helping with recipes and cooking directions. Thanks to my sister, Suthaseenee Jansala, and my dad, Sukit Jansala, for their comments, love and endless support.

ABOUT THE AUTHOR

Sarah Jansala is a co-founder and chef at Kati Portland, Thai Vegetarian Restaurant, and a founder of The Pear Café, Juice Bar and Thai Veg Café, both located in Portland, Oregon. She received her bachelor of science in biology from Middle Tennessee State University, and her doctor of pharmacy from University of Tennessee. Sarah currently works as a retail pharmacist and is licensed in the state of Oregon. Sarah is passionate about how balancing a healthy diet and good physical activity can lead to a healthier life.

INDEX

D

E

F

N

O

P

R

S

T

V

W

Y